Scotland Act 2016

CHAPTER 11

Explanatory Notes are available separately

GRAN*GIS* UK Publishing

Adapted and published by GRANGIS (Grand Register Library).
Online: www.grangis.com
E-mail: contact@grangis.com

In this version:
ISBN: 979-8-88559-032-7

Note: This is the original version (as it was originally enacted). Title, sub-title and the generated date is as marked on the pages.

Scotland Act 2016

CHAPTER 11

SCOTLAND ACT 2016

PART 1

CONSTITUTIONAL ARRANGEMENTS

The Scottish Parliament and the Scottish Government

1 Permanence of the Scottish Parliament and Scottish Government

The Sewel convention

2 The Sewel convention

Elections etc

3 Elections
4 Power to make provision about elections
5 Timing of elections
6 Electoral registration: the digital service
7 Expenditure in connection with elections
8 Review of electoral boundaries by the Local Government Boundary Commission for Scotland
9 Functions exercisable within devolved competence: elections
10 Minor and consequential amendments: elections etc

Legislation by the Parliament

11 Super-majority requirement for certain legislation
12 Scope to modify the Scotland Act 1998

PART 2

TAX, BORROWING AND FINANCIAL INFORMATION

Income tax

13 Power of Scottish Parliament to set rates of income tax
14 Amendments of Income Tax Act 2007
15 Consequential amendments: income tax

Value added tax

16 Assignment of VAT

Devolved taxes

17 Tax on carriage of passengers by air
18 Tax on commercial exploitation of aggregate
19 Devolved taxes: further provision

Borrowing

20 Borrowing

Information

21 Provision of information to the Office for Budget Responsibility

PART 3

WELFARE BENEFITS AND EMPLOYMENT SUPPORT

Welfare benefits

22 Disability, industrial injuries and carer's benefits
23 Benefits for maternity, funeral and heating expenses
24 Discretionary payments: top-up of reserved benefits
25 Discretionary housing payments
26 Discretionary payments and assistance
27 Welfare foods
28 Power to create other new benefits
29 Universal credit: costs of claimants who rent accommodation
30 Universal credit: persons to whom, and time when, paid

Employment support

31 Employment support

General

32 Functions exercisable within devolved competence
33 Social Security Advisory Committee and Industrial Injuries Advisory Council
34 Information-sharing
35 Extension of unauthorised disclosure offence

PART 4

OTHER LEGISLATIVE COMPETENCE

36 Crown Estate
37 Equal opportunities
38 Public sector duty regarding socio-economic inequalities
39 Tribunals
40 Roads
41 Roads: traffic signs etc
42 Roads: speed limits
43 Roads: parking
44 Roads: consequential provision etc
45 Policing of railways and railway property
46 British Transport Police: cross-border public authorities
47 Onshore petroleum
48 Onshore petroleum: consequential amendments
49 Onshore petroleum: existing licences
50 Consumer advocacy and advice
51 Functions exercisable within devolved competence: consumer advocacy and advice
52 Gaming machines on licensed betting premises
53 Abortion

PART 5

OTHER EXECUTIVE COMPETENCE

54 Gaelic Media Service
55 Commissioners of Northern Lighthouses
56 Maritime and Coastguard Agency
57 Rail: franchising of passenger services
58 Fuel poverty: support schemes
59 Energy company obligations
60 Apportionment of targets
61 Renewable electricity incentive schemes: consultation
62 Offshore renewable energy installations
63 References to Competition and Markets Authority

PART 6

MISCELLANEOUS

64 Gas and Electricity Markets Authority
65 Office of Communications
66 Bodies that may be required to attend before the Parliament
67 Destination of fines, forfeitures and fixed penalties

PART 7

GENERAL

68 Subordinate legislation under functions exercisable within devolved competence
69 Transfers of property etc to the Scottish Ministers
70 Transitional provision

71 Power to make consequential, transitional and saving provision
72 Commencement
73 Short title

SCHEDULES

SCHEDULE 1 — DISAPPLICATION OF UK AGGREGATES LEVY: FURTHER AMENDMENTS

1 Part 2 of The Finance Act 2001 (aggregates levy) is...
2 (1) Section 17 (meanings of "aggregate" and "taxable aggregate") is...
3 (1) Section 19 (commercial exploitation) is amended as follows.
4 In section 20(1)(a) (originating sites) for "the United Kingdom" substitute...
5 (1) Section 24 (levy register) is amended as follows.
6 In section 26(3) (offence of failing to provide security for...
7 (1) Section 30 (credit for aggregates levy) is amended as...
8 In section 44(a) (destination of receipts collected or received in...
9 In section 48(1) (interpretation of Part 2) in the definition...
10 In Schedule 4 (registration), in paragraph 8(2) (interpretation of references...
11 In Schedule 6 (evasion etc), in paragraph 4(1)(a) (preparations for...
12 (1) Schedule 7 (information and evidence etc) is amended as...
13 In Schedule 23 to the Finance Act 2011 (data-gathering powers...

SCHEDULE 2 — ROADS: CONSEQUENTIAL AND RELATED PROVISION

PART 1 — AMENDMENTS

1 Road Traffic Regulation Act 1984 (c. 52)
2 (1) Section 15 (duration of orders etc under section 14)...
3 (1) Section 16 (supplementary provision as to orders etc under...
4 In section 17 (traffic regulation on special roads)—
5 In section 24 (Secretary of State to establish crossings on...
6 In section 25(6)(b) (meaning of "crossing" in section 25 includes...
7 In section 28 (stopping of vehicles at school crossings) for...
8 (1) Section 86 (speed limits for particular classes of vehicles)...
9 In section 88 (temporary speed limits) for "national authority" in...
10 In section 124(1) (purposes of Schedule 9 etc) in paragraphs...
11 (1) Section 131 (application of road traffic enactments to Crown...
12 (1) Section 134 (regulations) is amended as follows.
13 In section 142(1) (general interpretation) omit the definition of "the...
14 (1) Part 1 of Schedule 9 (reserve powers of Secretary...
15 (1) Part 2 of Schedule 9 (consent of Secretary of...
16 (1) Part 3 of Schedule 9 (procedure as to certain...
17 (1) Part 4 of Schedule 9 (variation or revocation of...
18 In Part 5 of Schedule 9 (consultation with traffic commissioners),...
19 Road Traffic Act 1988 (c. 52)
20 Road Traffic (Temporary Restrictions) Procedure Regulations 1992 (S.I. 1992/1215)
21 In regulation 9(1) (continuation of order by direction of Secretary...
22 In regulation 15(5) (modification of regulation 9 in its application...
23 Zebra, Pelican and Puffin Pedestrian Crossings Regulations and General Directions 1997 (S.I. 1997/2400)
24 (1) Part 1 (the Zebra, Pelican and Puffin Pedestrian Crossings...

25 (1) Part 2 (the Pelican and Puffin Pedestrian Crossings General...
26 National Assembly for Wales (Transfer of Functions) Order 1999 (S.I. 1999/672)
27 Scotland Act 1998 (Transfer of Functions to the Scottish Ministers etc) Order 1999 (S.I. 1999/1750)
28 In Schedule 1 (enactments conferring functions transferred to the Scottish...
29 In Schedule 3 (enactments conferring functions to be exercised subject...
30 Traffic Signs Regulations and General Directions 2002 (S.I. 2002/3113)
31 In Part 1 (the Traffic Signs Regulations 2002), in regulation...
32 (1) Part 2 (the Traffic Signs General Directions) is amended...
33 Scotland Act 1998 (Transfer of Functions to the Scottish Ministers etc) Order 2005 (S.I. 2005/849)
PART 2 — EXERCISE OF POWERS BY AGREEMENT
34 Traffic Sign Powers
35 Powers to exempt from speed limits

Scotland Act 2016

2016 CHAPTER 11

An Act to amend the Scotland Act 1998 and make provision about the functions of the Scottish Ministers; and for connected purposes. [23rd March 2016]

BE IT ENACTED by the Queen's most Excellent Majesty, by and with the advice and consent of the Lords Spiritual and Temporal, and Commons, in this present Parliament assembled, and by the authority of the same, as follows:—

PART 1

CONSTITUTIONAL ARRANGEMENTS

The Scottish Parliament and the Scottish Government

1 Permanence of the Scottish Parliament and Scottish Government

In the Scotland Act 1998 after Part 2 (the Scottish Administration) insert—

"PART 2A

PERMANENCE OF THE SCOTTISH PARLIAMENT AND SCOTTISH GOVERNMENT

63A Permanence of the Scottish Parliament and Scottish Government

(1) The Scottish Parliament and the Scottish Government are a permanent part of the United Kingdom's constitutional arrangements.

(2) The purpose of this section is, with due regard to the other provisions of this Act, to signify the commitment of the Parliament and Government of the United Kingdom to the Scottish Parliament and the Scottish Government.

(3) In view of that commitment it is declared that the Scottish Parliament and the Scottish Government are not to be abolished except on the basis of a decision of the people of Scotland voting in a referendum."

The Sewel convention

2 The Sewel convention

In section 28 of the Scotland Act 1998 (Acts of the Scottish Parliament) at the end add—

"(8) But it is recognised that the Parliament of the United Kingdom will not normally legislate with regard to devolved matters without the consent of the Scottish Parliament."

Elections etc

3 Elections

(1) Section B3 of Part 2 of Schedule 5 to the Scotland Act 1998 (elections) is amended as follows.

(2) Under the heading "B3 Elections" insert—

(A) *"Elections for membership of the House of Commons and the European Parliament".*

(3) For ", the European Parliament and the Parliament" substitute "and the European Parliament".

(4) Omit the words from "The franchise at local government elections" to the end of the Exceptions and insert—

(B) *"Elections for membership of the Parliament and local government elections in Scotland*

The subject-matter of sections 2(2A) and 12A of this Act.

The subject-matter of section 43(1AA) of the Representation of the People Act 1983.

The combination of—

(a) polls at elections or referendums that are outside the legislative competence of the Parliament with polls at—

(i) elections for membership of the Parliament, or

(ii) local government elections in Scotland, and

(b) polls at ordinary general elections for membership of the Parliament with polls at ordinary local government elections in Scotland.

Any digital service provided by a Minister of the Crown for the registration of electors.

The subject matter of—

(a) Parts 5 and 6 of the Political Parties, Elections and Referendums Act 2000 (expenditure in connection with elections) where a limit applies to expenditure in relation to a period determined by reference both to the date of the poll for an election within the legislative competence of the Parliament and to the date of the poll at an election for membership of the House of Commons or the European Parliament, and

(b) sections 145 to 148 and 150 to 154 of that Act (enforcement) as they apply for the purposes of Part 5 or 6, so far as the subject-matter of that Part is reserved by paragraph (a).

The subject matter of—

(a) sections 155 and 156 of the Political Parties, Elections and Referendums Act 2000, except in relation to Parts 5 and 6 of that Act so far as those Parts relate to elections for membership of the Parliament, and

(b) sections 145 to 148 and 150 to 154 of that Act as they apply for the purposes of section 155 or 156, so far as the subject-matter of that section is reserved by paragraph (a).

The subject-matter of the following sections of the Political Parties, Elections and Referendums Act 2000 in relation to elections for membership of the Parliament—

(a) section 1, except in relation to—

(i) financing the Electoral Commission,

(ii) preparation, laying and publication by the Commission of reports about the performance of its functions, and

(iii) provision by the Commission of copies of regulations made by it or notice of the alteration or revocation of such regulations,

(b) sections 2 to 4, 6(1)(e) and (f) (and (g) to the extent that it relates to the law mentioned in those paragraphs),

(c) sections 12, 21 to 33, 35 to 37, 39 to 57, 58 to 67, 69, 71, 71F, 71G, 71H to 71Y and 140A,

(d) section 149 (except in relation to the register kept under section 89),

(e) sections 157 and 159 to 163, and

(f) sections 145 to 148 and 150 to 154 as they apply for the purposes of a provision mentioned in paragraphs (a) to (e), so far as the subject matter of that provision is reserved by those paragraphs."

(5) In the Interpretation provision, omit the definitions of "Digital service" and "Ordinary local election" and insert—

"Paragraph 5(1) of Part 3 of this Schedule does not apply to the subject-matter of the Political Parties, Elections and Referendums Act 2000; and references to the subject-matter of that Act are to be read as at the day on which the Scotland Act 2016 received Royal Assent."

4 Power to make provision about elections

(1) For sections 12 and 12A of the Scotland Act 1998 (power of Scottish Ministers and Secretary of State to make provision about elections) substitute—

"12 Power of the Scottish Ministers to make provision about elections

(1) The Scottish Ministers may by order make any provision that would be within the legislative competence of the Parliament, if included in an Act of the Scottish Parliament, as to—

(a) the conduct of elections for membership of the Parliament,

(b) the questioning of such an election and the consequences of irregularities, and

(c) the return of members of the Parliament otherwise than at an election.

(2) The provision that may be made under subsection (1)(a) includes, in particular, provision—

(a) about the registration of electors,

(b) for disregarding alterations in a register of electors,

(c) about the limitation of the election expenses of candidates,

(d) for the combination of polls,

(e) for modifying the application of section 7(1) where the poll at an election for the return of a constituency member is abandoned (or notice of it is countermanded), and

(f) for modifying section 8(7) to ensure the allocation of the correct number of seats for the region.

(3) The provision that may be made under subsection (1)(c) includes, in particular, provision modifying section 10(4) to (5A).

(4) An order under subsection (1) may—

(a) apply, with or without modifications or exceptions, any provision made by or under the Representation of the People Acts or the European Parliamentary Elections Act 2002 or by any other enactment relating to parliamentary elections, European Parliamentary elections or local government elections, and

(b) so far as may be necessary in consequence of any provision made by an order under subsection (1), modify any provision made by any enactment relating to the registration of parliamentary electors or local government electors.

(5) The return of a member of the Parliament at an election may be questioned only under Part 3 of the Representation of the People Act 1983 as applied by an order under subsection (1).

(6) For the purposes of this Act, the regional returning officer for any region is the person designated as such in accordance with an order made by the Scottish Ministers under this subsection.

12A Power of the Secretary of State to make provision about the combination of polls

(1) The Secretary of State may by regulations make provision for—

(a) the combination of polls at ordinary general elections for membership of the Parliament with polls at the elections listed in subsection (2), and

(b) the combination of polls at extraordinary general elections for membership of the Parliament, and by-elections for membership of the Parliament, with polls at the elections listed in subsections (2) and (3).

(2) The elections are—

(a) early parliamentary general elections,

(b) parliamentary by-elections, and

(c) European parliamentary by-elections.

(3) The elections are—

(a) parliamentary general elections, and

(b) European parliamentary general elections.

(4) The Secretary of State may not make regulations under this section without the agreement of the Scottish Ministers.

(5) Regulations under subsection (1) may—

(a) apply, with or without modifications or exceptions, any provision made by or under the Representation of the People Acts or the European Parliamentary Elections Act 2002 or by any other enactment relating to parliamentary elections, European Parliamentary elections or local government elections, and

(b) modify any form contained in, or in regulations or rules made under, the Representation of the People Acts so far as may be necessary to enable it to be used both for the original purpose and in relation to elections for membership of the Parliament."

(2) In section 15 of the Representation of the People Act 1985 (combination of polls) after subsection (5B) insert—

"(5C) Before making provision under subsection (5) in connection with the combination of polls where one of the elections is a local government election in Scotland, the Secretary of State must consult the Scottish Ministers."

5 Timing of elections

(1) Section 2 of the Scotland Act 1998 (ordinary general elections) is amended as follows.

(2) In subsection (2) for the words from "the day" to the end substitute—

"(a) subsection (2A) prevents the poll being held on that day, or

(b) the day of the poll is determined by a proclamation under subsection (5)."

(3) After subsection (2) insert—

"(2A) The poll shall not be held on the same date as the date of the poll at—

(a) a parliamentary general election (other than an early parliamentary general election), or

(b) a European parliamentary general election.

(2B) Where subsection (2A) prevents the poll being held on the day specified in subsection (2), the poll shall be held on such day, subject to subsection (2A), as the Scottish Ministers may by order specify, unless the day of the poll is determined by a proclamation under subsection (5) as modified by subsection (5ZA)."

(4) In subsection (3) after "May" insert ", or on the day specified by an order under subsection (2B)".

(5) In subsection (5) at the beginning insert "Subject to subsection (2A),".

(6) After subsection (5) insert—

"(5ZA) Where a day is specified by order under subsection (2B), subsection (5) applies as if the reference to the first Thursday in May were a reference to that day."

(7) Omit subsections (5A) to (5C).

(8) In paragraph 1(2) of Schedule 7 (procedure for subordinate legislation) in the appropriate place insert—

"Section 2(2B)	Type L"

(9) Section 43 of the Representation of the People Act 1983 (day of ordinary local elections in Scotland, and other timing provisions) is amended as follows.

(10) In subsection (1) at the beginning insert "Subject to subsection (1AA),".

(11) After subsection (1A) insert—

"(1AA) The poll shall not be held on the day specified in or fixed under subsection (1) where that day is the day of the poll at an ordinary general election for membership of the Scottish Parliament.

(1AB) Where subsection (1AA) prevents the poll being held on the day specified in or fixed under subsection (1), the poll is to be held on such other day as the Scottish Ministers may by order specify.

(1AC) An order under subsection (1AB) is subject to the affirmative procedure."

6 Electoral registration: the digital service

(1) The Representation of the People Act 1983 is amended as follows.

(2) In section 10ZC (registration of electors in Great Britain) at the end insert—

"(4) The power to make regulations under this section, so far as it is exercisable by a Minister of the Crown to make provision about a UK digital service in relation to elections in Scotland, is exercisable by the Scottish Ministers concurrently with that Minister.

(5) The power of the Scottish Ministers to make regulations by virtue of subsection (4) is exercisable in the same ways and subject to the same provisions as their power to make other regulations under this section, except that—

(a) the power is not exercisable without the agreement of a Minister of the Crown, and

(b) regulations made in exercise of the power are subject to the negative procedure.

(6) In this section—

"election in Scotland" means—

(a) an election for membership of the Scottish Parliament, or

(b) a local government election in Scotland;

"UK digital service" means a digital service provided by a Minister of the Crown for the registration of electors."

(3) In section 10ZD (registration of electors in Great Britain: alterations) at the end insert—

"(4) The power to make regulations under this section, so far as it is exercisable by a Minister of the Crown to make provision about a UK digital service in relation to elections in Scotland, is exercisable by the Scottish Ministers concurrently with that Minister.

(5) The power of the Scottish Ministers to make regulations by virtue of subsection (4) is exercisable in the same ways and subject to the same provisions as their power to make other regulations under this section, except that—

(a) the power is not exercisable without the agreement of a Minister of the Crown, and

(b) regulations made in exercise of the power are subject to the negative procedure.

(6) In this section "election in Scotland" and "UK digital service" have the same meaning as in section 10ZC."

(4) In section 53 (power to make regulations about registration etc) at the end insert—

"(9) The power to make regulations under this section, so far as it is exercisable by a Minister of the Crown to make provision about a UK digital service in relation to elections in Scotland, is exercisable by the Scottish Ministers concurrently with that Minister.

(10) The power of the Scottish Ministers to make regulations by virtue of subsection (9) is exercisable in the same ways and subject to the same provisions as their power to make other regulations under this section, except that—

(a) the power is not exercisable without the agreement of a Minister of the Crown, and

(b) regulations made in exercise of the power are subject to the negative procedure.

(11) In subsection (9)—

"election in Scotland" means—

(a) an election for membership of the Scottish Parliament, or

(b) a local government election in Scotland;

"UK digital service" means a digital service provided by a Minister of the Crown for the registration of electors."

7 Expenditure in connection with elections

(1) The Political Parties, Elections and Referendums Act 2000 is amended as follows.

(2) After section 72 (campaign expenditure) insert—

"72A Campaign expenditure: power of Scottish Ministers

(1) The powers under the following provisions of Schedule 8 are exercisable by the Scottish Ministers instead of the Secretary of State, so far as they relate to polls at elections for membership of the Scottish Parliament—

(a) paragraph 3(3) (power to approve a draft code of practice prepared by the Electoral Commission),

(b) paragraph 3(7) (power to appoint day when code comes into force), and

(c) paragraph 4(1) (power to amend Part 1 of Schedule 8).

(2) For the purposes of the exercise by the Scottish Ministers of the powers mentioned in subsection (1), paragraphs 3 and 4 of Schedule 8 apply—

(a) as if any reference to the Secretary of State were a reference to the Scottish Ministers,

(b) as if any reference to "each House of Parliament", "each House", "either House", "both Houses" or "Parliament" were a reference to the Scottish Parliament,

(c) as if in paragraph 3(9) for the words from "means—" to the end there were substituted "means the period of 40 days beginning with the day on which the draft is laid before the Scottish Parliament."

(3) Subsection (1) does not apply to a power so far as it relates to circumstances where a limit applies to expenditure in relation to a period determined by reference both to the date of the poll for an election for membership of the Scottish Parliament and to the date of any other election."

(3) After section 85 (controlled expenditure of third parties) insert—

"85A Controlled expenditure of third parties: power of Scottish Ministers

(1) The powers under the following provisions of Schedule 8A are exercisable by the Scottish Ministers instead of the Secretary of State, so far as they relate to polls at elections for membership of the Scottish Parliament—

(a) paragraph 3(3) (power to approve a draft code of practice prepared by the Electoral Commission),

(b) paragraph 3(7) (power to appoint day when code comes into force), and

(c) paragraph 4(1) (power to amend Part 1 of Schedule 8A).

(2) For the purposes of the exercise by the Scottish Ministers of the powers mentioned in subsection (1), paragraphs 3 and 4 of Schedule 8A apply—

(a) as if any reference to the Secretary of State were a reference to the Scottish Ministers,

(b) as if any reference to "each House of Parliament", "each House", "either House", "both Houses" or "Parliament" were a reference to the Scottish Parliament,

(c) as if in paragraph 3(9) for the words from "means—" to the end there were substituted "means the period of 40 days beginning with the day on which the draft is laid before the Scottish Parliament."

(3) Subsection (1) does not apply to a power so far as it relates to circumstances where a limit applies to expenditure in relation to a period determined by reference both to the date of the poll for an election for membership of the Scottish Parliament and to the date of any other election."

(4) After section 95 (control of donations to recognised third parties) insert—

"95ZA Control of donation to recognised third parties: power of Scottish Ministers

(1) The powers under the following provisions of Schedule 11 are exercisable by the Scottish Ministers instead of the Secretary of State, so far as they relate to polls at elections for membership of the Scottish Parliament—

(a) paragraph 3(4) (power to change meaning of defined expenses and sponsorship),

(b) paragraph 6A(6) (power to make regulations about how the value of a benefit is calculated), and

(c) paragraph 6B(4) (power to make regulations about the retention of declarations).

(2) For the purposes of the exercise by the Scottish Ministers of the powers mentioned in subsection (1), paragraphs 3, 6A and 6B of Schedule 11 apply as if any reference to the Secretary of State was a reference to the Scottish Ministers.

(3) Subsection (1) does not apply to a power so far as it relates to circumstances where a limit applies to expenditure in relation to a period determined by reference both to the date of the poll for an election for membership of the Scottish Parliament and to the date of any other election."

(5) Section 95ZA inserted by subsection (4) has effect—

(a) until the coming into force of paragraph 1(2) of Schedule 3 to the Political Parties and Elections Act 2009, with the omission of subsection (1)(b) and "6A" in subsection (2);

(b) until the coming into force of paragraph 4(2) of Schedule 4 to that Act, with the omission of subsection (1)(c) and "and 6B" in subsection (2).

(6) Section 155 (power to vary specified sums or percentages) is amended as follows.

(7) In subsection (1) at the beginning insert "Except where subsection (1A) applies,".

(8) After subsection (1) insert—

"(1A) The Scottish Ministers may by order vary any sum for the time being specified in Part 5 or 6 so far as that sum applies in relation to an election the conduct of which is within the legislative competence of the Scottish Parliament."

(9) In subsection (2)—

(a) for the words before paragraph (a) substitute "An order under subsection (1) or (1A) may be made either—", and

(b) in paragraph (a) for "he" substitute "the person making the order".

(10) After subsection (4) insert—

"(4A) Subsection (4B) applies in relation to the sums specified in Schedule 11.

(4B) In each session of the Scottish Parliament, other than a session that is dissolved less than two years after the date of its first sitting, the Scottish Ministers must either—

(a) make an order in pursuance of subsection (2)(a), or

(b) lay before the Scottish Parliament a statement setting out the Scottish Ministers' reasons for not doing so."

(11) Section 156 (orders and regulations) is amended as follows.

(12) After subsection (4A) insert—

"(4B) Subject to subsections (4C) and (4D), any order or regulations made under this Act by the Scottish Ministers shall be subject to the negative procedure (see section 28 of the Interpretation and Legislative Reform (Scotland) Act 2010).

(4C) Subsection (4B) does not apply to an order falling within subsection (3).

(4D) Subsection (4B) does not apply to an order falling within subsection (4), and any such order made by the Scottish Ministers shall be subject to the affirmative procedure (see section 29 of the Interpretation and Legislative Reform (Scotland) Act 2010)."

(13) In subsection (5) after each "Secretary of State" insert "or the Scottish Ministers".

(14) In the Interpretation and Legislative Reform (Scotland) Act 2010, in section 30(4) (other instruments laid before the Parliament: exceptions) after paragraph (f) insert—

"(fa) section 155(2)(a) of the Political Parties, Elections and Referendums Act 2000 (c.41),".

8 Review of electoral boundaries by the Local Government Boundary Commission for Scotland

(1) Schedule 1 to the Scotland Act 1998 is amended as follows.

(2) For "the Boundary Commission for Scotland" in each place substitute "the Local Government Boundary Commission for Scotland".

(3) In paragraphs 3 to 7 for "the Secretary of State" in each place, and for "he" in paragraphs 3(9) and 6(1), substitute "the Scottish Ministers".

(4) In paragraphs 3 to 7 for—

(a) "each House of Parliament", "either House of Parliament" or "the House" in each place, and

(b) "Parliament" in all other places, except in paragraph 6(7),

substitute "the Parliament".

(5) In paragraph 3(4)—

(a) before "under this paragraph" insert "to the Scottish Ministers";

(b) for "not later than 30 June 2010" substitute "no earlier than 1 May 2018 and no later than 1 May 2022".

(6) In paragraph 3(6) omit "(but not before the submission of their first report)".

(7) Omit paragraph 3(11).

(8) In paragraph 6(1) for "thinks" substitute "think".

9 Functions exercisable within devolved competence: elections

(1) The Scotland Act 1998 ("the 1998 Act") has effect, in relation to any function so far as exercisable within devolved competence by virtue of a provision of section 3, as if references to a "pre-commencement enactment" were to—

(a) an Act passed before or in the same session as the relevant date,

(b) any other enactment made before the relevant date,

(c) subordinate legislation under section 106 of the 1998 Act, to the extent that the legislation states that it is to be treated as a pre-commencement enactment,

but did not include the 1998 Act or this Act (or any amendment made by either of those Acts) or (subject to paragraph (c)) an enactment comprised in subordinate legislation under either of those Acts.

(2) In this section—

(a) expressions used in the 1998 Act have the same meaning as in that Act;

(b) the relevant date is the date on which section 3 comes into force.

10 Minor and consequential amendments: elections etc

(1) This section makes minor and consequential amendments in relation to elections and related matters.

(2) The Scotland Act 1998 is amended as follows.

(3) Omit sections 92(4A), 104(3) and 112(6) and paragraph 11(4) of Schedule 4 (functions under section 15 to be regarded as exercisable within devolved competence).

(4) In Schedule 4, omit paragraph 4(2A) and (2B) (voting age), and (2C) (date of elections to the Parliament).

(5) In Part 1 of Schedule 5, omit paragraph 5A (referendums).

(6) In the Scotland Act 2012, omit sections 1, 2 and 13.

(7) The Scotland Act 1998 (Modification of Schedules 4 and 5 and Transfer of Functions to the Scottish Ministers) Order 2015 (S.I. 2015/692) and the Scotland Act 1998 (Modification of Schedules 4 and 5) Order 2015 (S.I. 2015/1764) are revoked.

Legislation by the Parliament

11 Super-majority requirement for certain legislation

(1) The Scotland Act 1998 is amended as follows.

(2) Section 31 (scrutiny of Bills before introduction) is amended as follows.

(3) In the heading for "before introduction" substitute "for legislative competence and protected subject-matter".

(4) After subsection (2) insert—

"(2A) The Presiding Officer shall, after the last time when a Bill may be amended but before the decision whether to pass or reject it, decide whether or not in his view any provision of the Bill relates to a protected subject-matter and state his decision."

(5) At the end insert—

"(4) For the purposes of this Part a provision of a Bill relates to a protected subject-matter if it would modify, or confer power to modify, any of the matters listed in subsection (5) (but not if the provision is incidental to or consequential on another provision of the Bill).

(5) The matters are—

(a) the persons entitled to vote as electors at an election for membership of the Parliament,

(b) the system by which members of the Parliament are returned,

(c) the number of constituencies, regions or any equivalent electoral area, and

(d) the number of members to be returned for each constituency, region or equivalent electoral area."

(6) After that section insert—

"31A Two-thirds majority for Bills relating to a protected subject-matter

If the Presiding Officer states under section 31(2A) that in his view any provision of a Bill relates to a protected subject-matter, the Bill is not passed unless the number of members voting in favour of it at the final stage is at least two-thirds of the total number of seats for members of the Parliament."

(7) Section 32 (submission of Bills for Royal Assent) is amended as follows.

(8) In subsection (2)(a) after "under section" insert "32A or".

(9) After subsection (2) insert—

"(2A) The Presiding Officer shall not submit a Bill for Royal Assent if the Supreme Court has decided on a reference made in relation to the Bill under section 32A(2)(b) that any provision of the Bill relates to a protected subject-matter, unless since the decision the Bill has been approved in accordance with standing orders made by virtue of section 36(5)."

(10) After that section insert—

"32A Scrutiny of Bills by the Supreme Court (protected subject-matter)

(1) The Advocate General, the Lord Advocate or the Attorney General may refer the question of whether a Bill or any provision of a Bill relates to a protected subject-matter to the Supreme Court for decision.

(2) Subject to subsection (3), he may make a reference in relation to a Bill—

(a) at any time during the period of four weeks beginning with the rejection of the Bill, if the Presiding Officer has made a statement under section 31(2A) that in his view any provision of the Bill relates to a protected subject-matter, and

(b) at any time during the period of four weeks beginning with the passing of the Bill, if the Presiding Officer has made a statement under section 31(2A) that in his view no provision of the Bill relates to a protected subject-matter, unless the number of members voting in favour of the Bill at its passing is at least two-thirds of the total number of seats for members of the Parliament.

(3) He shall not make a reference in relation to a Bill if he has notified the Presiding Officer that he does not intend to make a reference in relation to the Bill, unless since the notification the Bill has been approved or rejected in accordance with standing orders made by virtue of section 36(5)."

(11) Section 33 (scrutiny of Bills by the Supreme Court) is amended as follows.

(12) In the heading after "Supreme Court" insert "(legislative competence)".

(13) In subsection (2)(b) omit "subsequent".

(14) In section 35(3) (power to intervene in certain cases)—

(a) in paragraph (b) omit "subsequent", and

(b) in paragraph (c) after "section" insert "32A(2)(b) or".

(15) Section 36 (stages of Bills) is amended as follows.

(16) In subsection (4) after paragraph (a) insert—

"(aa) the Supreme Court decides on a reference made in relation to the Bill under section 32A(2)(b) that any provision of the Bill relates to a protected subject-matter,".

(17) After that subsection insert—

"(4A) Standing orders shall provide for an opportunity for the reconsideration of a Bill after its rejection if (and only if), on a reference made in relation to the Bill under section 32A(2)(a), the Supreme Court decides that no provision that is subject to the reference relates to a protected subject-matter."

(18) In subsection (5) for "any Bill amended on reconsideration" substitute "—

(a) any Bill amended on reconsideration in accordance with standing orders made by virtue of subsection (4)(a), (b) or (c), and

(b) any Bill reconsidered in accordance with standing orders made by virtue of subsection (4)(aa) or (4A),".

(19) In subsection (6)—

"(a) after "28(2)" insert ", 31(2A), 31A, 32A(2)(b)";

(b) for "which has been amended on reconsideration" substitute "to which subsection (5)(a) or (b) applies".

12 Scope to modify the Scotland Act 1998

(1) The Scotland Act 1998 is amended as follows.

(2) In paragraph 4 of Schedule 4 (protection of Scotland Act 1998 from modification) for sub-paragraph (2) substitute—

"(2) This paragraph does not apply to modifying—

(a) the following sections in Part 1 (the Scottish Parliament)—

(i) section 1(2) to (5),

(ii) section 2(1), (2), (2B) and (3) to (6),

(iii) sections 3 to 12,

(iv) sections 13 to 22,

(v) sections 24 to 26,

(vi) section 27(1) and (2),

(vii) section 28(4) and (5),

(viii) section 31(3),

(ix) section 36(1)(a) and (b), and (2) and (3), and

(x) sections 38 to 42,

(b) the following sections in Part 2 (the Scottish Administration)—

(i) section 44(1)(a) to (c) and (2),

(ii) section 45(3) to (7),

(iii) section 46(1) to (3),

(iv) section 47(2) and (3)(b) to (e),

(v) section 48(2) to (4),

(vi) section 49(2), (3) and (4)(b) to (e), and

(vii) section 50,

(c) in Part 3 (financial provisions)—

(i) section 69(2) to (5), and

(ii) section 70(1) to (5) and (7) to (9),

(d) in Part 5 (miscellaneous and general), sections 81 to 83, 85, 91, 92(1), (2) and (4) to (6), 93, 94 and 97,

(e) the following provisions in Part 6 (supplementary)—

(i) section 112(1) and (3) to (5), section 113 (except the application of subsection (9)), section 115 and Schedule 7 (so far as those sections and that Schedule apply to any power exercisable within devolved competence to make subordinate legislation),

(ii) sections 118, 120 and 121, and

(iii) section 124 (so far as that section applies to any power exercisable within devolved competence to make subordinate legislation),

(f) Schedule 1 (constituencies, regions and regional members),

(g) paragraphs 1, 2(1) and 3 to 6 of Schedule 2 (Scottish Parliamentary corporate body), and

(h) paragraphs 1 to 6 of Schedule 3 (standing orders - further provision)."

(3) In paragraph 1 of Schedule 7 (procedure for subordinate legislation) in the entry for section 97 for "Type A" substitute "Type D".

PART 2

TAX, BORROWING AND FINANCIAL INFORMATION

Income tax

13 Power of Scottish Parliament to set rates of income tax

(1) Section 80C of the Scotland Act 1998 (power to set a Scottish rate for Scottish taxpayers) is amended as follows.

(2) In subsection (1) (power to set Scottish rate) for the words from "the Scottish rate" to the end substitute "the Scottish basic rate, and any other rates, for the purposes of section 11A of the Income Tax Act 2007 (which provides for the income of Scottish taxpayers which is charged at those rates)".

(3) For subsection (2) substitute—

"(2A) Where a Scottish rate resolution sets more than one rate it must also set limits or make other provision to enable it to be ascertained, for the purposes of that section, which rates apply in relation to a Scottish taxpayer.

(2B) But a Scottish rate resolution may not provide for different rates to apply in relation to different types of income.

(2C) In this Chapter a "Scottish rate" means a rate set by a Scottish rate resolution."

(4) Omit subsection (4).

(5) In subsection (5) (Scottish rate to be a whole number or half a whole number)—

(a) for "The" substitute "A", and

(b) at the end insert ", or zero".

(6) In the title for "rate" substitute "rates".

(7) Other provisions of Part 4A of the Scotland Act 1998 are amended as follows.

(8) In section 80A(1)(a) (overview of Part 4A) after "rate" insert "or rates".

(9) Section 80G (supplemental powers to modify enactments) is amended as follows.

(10) In subsection (1) (power to modify section 11A of the Income Tax Act 2007)—

(a) in the words before paragraph (a) for "the Scottish basic, higher and additional" substitute "Scottish", and

(b) in paragraph (a) for "the rates provided for under the section" substitute "Scottish rates".

(11) In subsection (1A) (power to modify references to certain rates of income tax in relation to Scottish taxpayers) for the words after "enactment" substitute "so as to make any provision that they consider necessary or expedient in consequence of or in connection with—

(a) the powers of the Parliament under section 80C;

(b) a Scottish rate resolution".

(12) In subsection (1B) (power to postpone effect of Scottish rate etc in relation to PAYE regulations) for paragraphs (a) and (b) substitute—

"(a) provision made by a Scottish rate resolution for a tax year,
(b) the absence of particular provision in a Scottish rate resolution for a tax year, or
(c) the absence of a Scottish rate resolution for a tax year,".

(13) In section 80HA(3)(b) (report by the Comptroller and Auditor General: meaning of "Scottish rate provisions") for the words from "the Scottish basic rate" to the end substitute "a Scottish rate".

(14) This section comes into force on such day as the Treasury may by regulations appoint.

(15) The amendments made by this section have effect in relation to the tax year appointed by the Treasury by regulations and subsequent tax years.

(16) The tax year appointed under subsection (15) must begin on or after the day appointed under subsection (14).

(17) Regulations under this section must be made by statutory instrument.

14 Amendments of Income Tax Act 2007

(1) The Income Tax Act 2007 is amended as follows.

(2) Section 6 (rates at which income tax is charged) is amended as follows.

(3) In subsection (3) omit paragraph (za).

(4) After that subsection insert—

"(4) See also section 80C of the Scotland Act 1998 which makes provision for the purposes of section 11A (income charged at Scottish rates)."

(5) Omit section 6A (the Scottish basic, higher and additional rates).

(6) In section 10(4) for "the Scottish basic, higher and additional" substitute "Scottish".

(7) Section 11A (income charged at the Scottish basic, higher and additional rates) is amended as follows.

(8) For subsections (1) to (3) substitute—

"(1A) Income tax is charged at Scottish rates on the non-savings income of a Scottish taxpayer."

(9) In subsection (6) for the words after "determining" substitute "which part of a Scottish taxpayer's income consists of savings income".

(10) In the title for "the Scottish basic, higher and additional" substitute "Scottish".

(11) In section 13 (income charged at dividend rates)—
(a) in subsection (1)(b) omit "or the Scottish basic rate,",
(b) in subsection (2)(b) omit "or the Scottish higher rate,",
(c) in subsection (2A)(b) omit "or the Scottish additional rate,",
(d) in subsection (4) omit "or the Scottish basic, higher or additional rate", and
(e) after subsection (4) insert—

"(5) In relation to an individual who is a Scottish taxpayer, references in this section to income that would otherwise be charged at a particular rate are to be read as references to income that would, if the individual were not a Scottish taxpayer, be charged at that rate (and subsection (4) is to be read accordingly)."

(12) For section 16(1)(za) (purposes for which section 16 has effect in relation to income tax of a Scottish taxpayer) substitute—

"(za) which part of a Scottish taxpayer's income consists of savings income,".

(13) In section 989 (definitions for the purposes of the Income Tax Acts)—

(a) omit the definitions of "Scottish additional rate" and "Scottish higher rate",

(b) in the definition of "Scottish basic rate", for the words after "Scottish basic rate" substitute "in relation to a tax year, means the Scottish basic rate set by a Scottish rate resolution for that year", and

(c) at the appropriate place insert—

""Scottish rate" in relation to a tax year, means a rate set by a Scottish rate resolution for that year,", and

""Scottish rate resolution" means a resolution of the Scottish Parliament under section 80C of the Scotland Act 1998,".

(14) In Schedule 4 (index of defined expressions)—

(a) omit the entries relating to the Scottish additional rate and the Scottish higher rate,

(b) in the entry relating to the Scottish basic rate for "6A (as applied by section 989)" substitute "989",

(c) at the appropriate place insert—

"Scottish rate	section 989"

(d) at the appropriate place insert—

"Scottish rate resolution	section 989"

(15) The amendments made by this section—

(a) come into force on the day appointed by the Treasury under section 13(14), and

(b) have effect in relation to the tax year appointed by the Treasury under section 13(15) and subsequent tax years.

15 Consequential amendments: income tax

(1) In section 110(2) of the Scotland Act 1998 (Scottish taxpayers: rates of income tax for social security purposes) for the words from "the Scottish basic rate" to "Scottish taxpayers" substitute "a Scottish rate (within the meaning of the Income Tax Acts)".

(2) Section 4 of the Taxation of Chargeable Gains Act 1992 (rates of capital gains tax) is amended as follows.

(3) In subsections (4) and (5) omit ", the Scottish higher rate".

(4) At the end insert—

"(10) For the purposes of the following references, an individual who is a Scottish taxpayer is to be treated as if the individual were not a Scottish taxpayer—

(a) the references in subsections (4) and (5) to income tax being chargeable at the higher rate;

(b) the reference in subsection (7) to the basic rate limit.

(11) Section 4A(5) is to be read accordingly."

(5) In section 4A(5) of that Act (section 4: special cases) omit ", the Scottish higher rate".

(6) In consequence of the amendments made by sections 13, 14 and this section omit the following provisions of Schedule 38 to the Finance Act 2014—

(a) paragraph 2(b);

(b) paragraph 3;

(c) paragraph 6(a) to (c) and (e);

(d) paragraph 7;

(e) paragraph 15(2) and (3);

(f) paragraph 16(2) and (8).

(7) The amendments made by this section—

(a) come into force on the day appointed by the Treasury under section 13(14), and

(b) have effect in relation to the tax year appointed by the Treasury under section 13(15) and subsequent tax years.

(8) The Treasury may by regulations make—

(a) such consequential provision as they consider appropriate in connection with any provision of section 13 or 14;

(b) such transitional or saving provision as they consider appropriate in connection with the coming into force of any provision of section 13 or 14 or subsections (1) to (6).

(9) Regulations under this section may amend, repeal, revoke or otherwise modify an enactment, whenever passed or made (including this Act).

(10) The following are subject to any provision made by virtue of subsection (8)(b)—

(a) subsection (7);

(b) section 13(15);

(c) section 14(15).

(11) Regulations under this section must be made by statutory instrument.

(12) A statutory instrument containing regulations under this section which includes provision amending or repealing a provision of an Act may not be made unless a draft of the instrument has been laid before and approved by a resolution of the House of Commons.

(13) Any other statutory instrument containing regulations under this section, if made without a draft having been approved by a resolution of the House of Commons, is subject to annulment in pursuance of a resolution of the House of Commons.

(14) In this section "enactment" includes an enactment contained in subordinate legislation (within the meaning of the Interpretation Act 1978).

Value added tax

16 Assignment of VAT

(1) The Scotland Act 1998 is amended as follows.

(2) In section 64 (Scottish Consolidated Fund), after subsection (2) insert—

"(2A) The Secretary of State shall in accordance with section 64A pay into the Fund out of money provided by Parliament any amounts payable under that section."

(3) After that section insert—

"64A Assignment of VAT

(1) Where there is an agreement between the Treasury and the Scottish Ministers for identifying an amount agreed to represent the standard rate VAT attributable to Scotland for any period ("the agreed standard rate amount"), the amount described in subsection (3) is payable under this section in respect of that period.

(2) Where there is an agreement between the Treasury and the Scottish Ministers for identifying an amount agreed to represent the reduced rate VAT attributable to Scotland for that period ("the agreed reduced rate amount"), the amount described in subsection (4) is payable under this section in respect of that period.

(3) The amount payable in accordance with subsection (1) is the amount obtained by multiplying the agreed standard rate amount by—

$$\frac{10}{SR}$$

where SR is the number of percentage points in the rate at which value added tax is charged under section 2(1) of the Value Added Tax Act 1994 for the period.

(4) The amount payable in accordance with subsection (2) is the amount obtained by multiplying the agreed reduced rate amount by—

$$\frac{2.5}{RR}.$$

where RR is the number of percentage points in the rate at which value added tax is charged under section 29A(1) of the Value Added Tax Act 1994 for the period.

(5) The payment of those amounts under section 64(2A) is to be made in accordance with any agreement between the Treasury and the Scottish Ministers as to the time of the payment or otherwise."

(4) The Commissioners for Revenue and Customs Act 2005 is amended as follows.

(5) In subsection (2) of section 18 (confidentiality: exceptions) omit "or" after paragraph (i), and after paragraph (j) insert ", or

(k) which is made in connection with (or with anything done with a view to) the making or implementation of an agreement referred to in section 64A(1) or (2) of the Scotland Act 1998 (assignment of VAT)."

(6) After that subsection insert—

"(2A) Information disclosed in reliance on subsection (2)(k) may not be further disclosed without the consent of the Commissioners (which may be general or specific)."

(7) In section 19 (wrongful disclosure) in subsections (1) and (8) after "18(1)" insert "or (2A)".

Devolved taxes

17 Tax on carriage of passengers by air

(1) In Part 4A of the Scotland Act 1998, after Chapter 4 insert—

"CHAPTER 5

TAX ON CARRIAGE OF PASSENGERS BY AIR

80L Tax on carriage of passengers by air

A tax charged on the carriage of passengers by air from airports in Scotland is a devolved tax."

(2) Tax may not be charged in accordance with that provision on the carriage of passengers boarding aircraft before the date appointed under subsection (7).

(3) Chapter 4 of Part 1 of The Finance Act 1994 (air passenger duty) is amended as follows.

(4) In section 28(4) (a chargeable passenger is a passenger whose journey begins at an airport in the United Kingdom), for "the United Kingdom" substitute "England, Wales or Northern Ireland".

(5) In section 31(4B) (exception for passengers departing from airports in designated region of the United Kingdom) for "the United Kingdom" substitute "England, Wales or Northern Ireland".

(6) The Air Passenger Duty (Designated Region of the United Kingdom) Order 2001 (S.I. 2001/808) is revoked.

(7) Subsections (3) to (6) have effect in relation to flights beginning on or after such date as the Treasury appoint by regulations made by statutory instrument.

18 Tax on commercial exploitation of aggregate

(1) In Part 4A of the Scotland Act 1998, after the Chapter 5 inserted by section 17 insert—

"CHAPTER 6

TAX ON COMMERCIAL EXPLOITATION OF AGGREGATE

80M Tax on commercial exploitation of aggregate

(1) A tax which is charged on aggregate when it is subjected to commercial exploitation in Scotland is a devolved tax.

(2) The tax must not be chargeable when aggregate is subjected to commercial exploitation for fuel.

(3) Aggregate is subjected to commercial exploitation for fuel—

(a) when the aggregate is used as fuel;

(b) when the aggregate is subjected to commercial exploitation for the purpose of extracting or producing anything capable of being used as fuel;

(c) when the aggregate becomes subject to an agreement to use it as mentioned in paragraph (a) or to subject it to commercial exploitation as mentioned in paragraph (b)."

(2) Tax may not be charged in accordance with that provision on commercial exploitation of aggregate which takes place before the date appointed under subsection (4).

(3) In section 16(2) of the Finance Act 2001 (aggregates levy) for "the United Kingdom" substitute "England, Wales or Northern Ireland".

(4) Subsection (3) and Schedule 1 (further amendments relating to the disapplication of UK aggregates levy to Scotland) have effect in relation to commercial exploitation of aggregate which takes place on or after such date as the Treasury appoint in regulations made by statutory instrument.

19 Devolved taxes: further provision

(1) In section 80A of the Scotland Act 1998 (overview of Part 4A), in subsection (1)(b), for "Chapters 3 and 4" substitute "The remaining Chapters".

(2) The Treasury may by regulations make further provision relating to—

(a) the disapplication of air passenger duty in relation to flights beginning at airports in Scotland;

(b) the disapplication of aggregates levy in relation to commercial exploitation of aggregate in Scotland.

(3) The power conferred by subsection (2) includes power—

(a) to make transitional or saving provision in connection with the coming into force of section 17 or 18 or Schedule 1;

(b) to amend, repeal, revoke or otherwise modify an enactment, whenever passed or made (including this Act).

(4) Section 17(7) and section 18(4) are subject to any provision made by virtue of subsection (3).

(5) Regulations under this section must be made by statutory instrument.

(6) A statutory instrument containing regulations under this section which includes provision amending or repealing a provision of an Act may not be made unless a draft of the instrument has been laid before and approved by a resolution of the House of Commons.

(7) Any other statutory instrument containing regulations under this section, if made without a draft having been approved by a resolution of the House of Commons, is subject to annulment in pursuance of a resolution of the House of Commons.

(8) In this section "enactment" includes an enactment contained in subordinate legislation (within the meaning of the Interpretation Act 1978).

Borrowing

20 Borrowing

(1) The Scotland Act 1998 is amended as follows.

(2) Section 66(1) (borrowing by the Scottish Ministers from the Secretary of State) is amended as follows.

(3) At the end of paragraph (b) omit "and".

(4) In paragraph (c)—

(a) after "devolved taxes," omit "or";

(b) after "Scottish rate resolution," insert "or from amounts payable under section 64A,".

(5) After paragraph (c) insert—

"(d) any sums which in accordance with rules determined by the Treasury are required by them to meet current expenditure because of an excess of welfare payments over forecast welfare payments, and

(e) any sums which in accordance with rules made by the Treasury are required by them to meet current expenditure because of a Scotland-specific negative economic shock."

(6) After that subsection insert—

"(1ZA) In subsection (1)(d) "welfare payments" means—

(a) payments under any provision relating to matters within exceptions 1 to 10 in Section F1 of Part 2 of Schedule 5 or exception 1 in Section H3 of that Part, and

(b) payments attributable to regulations made by the Scottish Ministers by virtue of section 29 or 30 of the Scotland Act 2016 (powers in relation to universal credit)."

(7) In section 67(2) and (3A) (lending under section 66(1)) for "£500 million" substitute "£1.75 billion".

(8) In section 67A (lending for capital expenditure) in subsections (1) and (3) for "£2.2 billion" substitute "£3 billion".

(9) The Treasury may by regulations make transitional or saving provision in connection with the coming into force of the amendments made by this section.

(10) Regulations under subsection (9) must be made by statutory instrument.

(11) A statutory instrument containing regulations under subsection (9), if made without a draft having been approved by a resolution of the House of Commons, is subject to annulment in pursuance of a resolution of the House of Commons.

Information

21 Provision of information to the Office for Budget Responsibility

(1) The Scotland Act 1998 is amended as follows.

(2) After section 96 (provision of information to the Treasury) insert—

"96A Provision of information to the Office for Budget Responsibility

(1) The Office for Budget Responsibility has a right of access at any reasonable time to all Scottish public finances information which it may reasonably require for the purpose of the performance of its duty under section 4 of the Budget Responsibility and National Audit Act 2011 (duty to examine and report on the sustainability of the public finances).

(2) The Office is entitled to require from any person holding or accountable for any Scottish public finances information any assistance or explanation which the Office reasonably thinks necessary for that purpose.

(3) "Scottish public finances information" means information held by the Scottish Ministers or by any Scottish public authority specified in regulations made by the Secretary of State.

(4) This section is subject to any enactment or rule of law which operates to prohibit or restrict the disclosure of information or the giving of any assistance or explanation."

(3) In Schedule 7 (procedure for subordinate legislation), in paragraph 1(2) insert at the appropriate place—

"Section 96A	Type C"

PART 3

WELFARE BENEFITS AND EMPLOYMENT SUPPORT

Welfare benefits

22 Disability, industrial injuries and carer's benefits

(1) In Part 2 of Schedule 5 to the Scotland Act 1998, Section F1 (social security schemes) is amended as follows.

(2) In the Exceptions, before the paragraph beginning "The subject-matter of Part II of the Social Work (Scotland) Act 1968" insert—

"**Exception 1**

Any of the following benefits—

(a) disability benefits, other than severe disablement benefit or industrial injuries benefits,

(b) severe disablement benefit, so far as payable in respect of a relevant person, and

(c) industrial injuries benefits, so far as relating to relevant employment or to participation in training for relevant employment;

but this exception does not except a benefit which is, or which is an element of, an excluded benefit.

Exception 2

Carer's benefits, other than a benefit which is, or which is an element of, an excluded benefit."

(3) In the Exceptions, at the beginning of the paragraph beginning "The subject-matter of Part II of the Social Work (Scotland) Act 1968" insert—

"**Exception 3**".

(4) In the Interpretation provision, after "local taxes." insert—

""Disability benefit" means a benefit which is normally payable in respect of—

(a) a significant adverse effect that impairment to a person's physical or mental condition has on his or her ability to carry out day-to-day activities (for example, looking after yourself, moving around or communicating), or

(b) a significant need (for example, for attention or for supervision to avoid substantial danger to anyone) arising from impairment to a person's physical or mental condition;

and for this purpose the adverse effect or need must not be short-term.

"Severe disablement benefit" means a benefit which is normally payable in respect of—

(a) a person's being incapable of work for a period of at least 28 weeks beginning not later than the person's 20th birthday, or

(b) a person's being incapable of work and disabled for a period of at least 28 weeks;

and "relevant person", in relation to severe disablement benefit, means a person who is entitled to severe disablement allowance under section 68 of the Social Security Contributions and Benefits Act 1992 on the date on which section 22 of the Scotland Act 2016 comes into force as respects severe disablement benefit.

"Industrial injuries benefit" means a benefit which is normally payable in respect of—

(a) a person's having suffered personal injury caused by accident arising out of and in the course of his or her employment, or

(b) a person's having developed a disease or personal injury due to the nature of his or her employment;

and for this purpose "employment" includes participation in training for employment.

"Relevant employment", in relation to industrial injuries benefit, means employment which—

(a) is employed earner's employment for the purposes of section 94 of the Social Security Contributions and Benefits Act 1992 as at 28 May 2015 (the date of introduction into Parliament of the Bill for the Scotland Act 2016), or

(b) would be such employment but for—

(i) the contract purporting to govern the employment being void, or

(ii) the person concerned not being lawfully employed,

as a result of a contravention of, or non-compliance with, provision in or made by virtue of an enactment passed to protect employees.

"Carer's benefit" means a benefit which is normally payable in respect of the regular and substantial provision of care by a person to a disabled person; and for this purpose "disabled person" means a person to whom a disability benefit is normally payable.

"Excluded benefit" means—

(a) a benefit, entitlement to which, or the amount of which, is normally determined to any extent by reference to a person's income or capital (for example, universal credit under Part 1 of the Welfare Reform Act 2012),

(b) a benefit which is payable out of the National Insurance Fund (for example, employment and support allowance under section 1(2)(a) of the Welfare Reform Act 2007), or

(c) a benefit payable by way of lump sum in respect of a person's having, or having had—

(i) pneumoconiosis,

(ii) byssinosis,

(iii) diffuse mesothelioma,

(iv) bilateral diffuse pleural thickening, or

(v) primary carcinoma of the lung where there is accompanying evidence of one or both of asbestosis and bilateral diffuse pleural thickening.

"Employment" includes any trade, business, profession, office or vocation (and "employed" is to be read accordingly)."

23 Benefits for maternity, funeral and heating expenses

(1) In Part 2 of Schedule 5 to the Scotland Act 1998, Section F1 is amended as follows.

(2) In the Exceptions, after exception 3 (see section 22(3) above) insert—

"**Exception 4**

Providing financial or other assistance for the purposes of meeting or reducing—

(a) maternity expenses,

(b) funeral expenses, or

(c) expenses for heating in cold weather."

(3) In the Exceptions, for the words from "But the following are not excepted" to "Act 2000 (discretionary housing payments)." substitute—

"**Exclusions from exceptions 1 to 10**

Nothing in exceptions 1 to 10 is to be read as excepting—

(a) the National Insurance Fund,

(b) the Social Fund, or

(c) the provision by a Minister of the Crown of assistance by way of loan for the purpose of meeting, or helping to meet, an intermittent expense."

(4) In the Interpretation provision, omit the words from "Paragraph 5(1) of Part 3 of this Schedule" to "it is to be treated as if it were."

(5) In section 138 of the Social Security Contributions and Benefits Act 1992 (payments out of the social fund) after subsection (4) insert—

"(4A) This section has effect in or as regards Scotland as if—

(a) references in subsections (1)(a) and (2) to the making of payments out of the social fund were to the making of payments by the Scottish Ministers,

(b) the reference in subsection (2) to the Secretary of State were to the Scottish Ministers, and

(c) the reference in subsection (4) to regulations were to regulations made by the Scottish Ministers.

(4B) Where regulations are made by the Scottish Ministers under this section—

(a) sections 175(2) and (7) and 176 do not apply, and

(b) the regulations are subject to the negative procedure (see section 28 of the Interpretation and Legislative Reform (Scotland) Act 2010).

(4C) The power to make an Order in Council under section 30(3) of the Scotland Act 1998 is exercisable for the purposes of this section as it is exercisable for the purposes of that Act."

24 Discretionary payments: top-up of reserved benefits

In Section F1 of Part 2 of Schedule 5 to the Scotland Act 1998, in the Exceptions, after exception 4 (see section 23 above) insert—

"**Exception 5**

Providing financial assistance to an individual who—

(a) is entitled to a reserved benefit, and

(b) appears to require financial assistance, in addition to any amount the individual receives by way of reserved benefit, for the purpose, or one of the purposes, for which the benefit is being provided.

This exception does not except discretionary financial assistance in a reserved benefit.

This exception also does not except providing financial assistance to meet or help to meet housing costs (as to which, see exception 6).

This exception also does not except providing financial assistance where the requirement for it arises from reduction, non-payability or suspension of a reserved benefit as a result of an individual's conduct (for example, non-compliance with work-related requirements relating to the benefit) unless—

(a) the requirement for it also arises from some exceptional event or exceptional circumstances, and

(b) the requirement for it is immediate.

For the purposes of this exception "reserved benefit" means a benefit which is to any extent a reserved matter."

25 Discretionary housing payments

In Section F1 of Part 2 of Schedule 5 to the Scotland Act 1998, in the Exceptions, after exception 5 (see section 24 above) insert—

"Exception 6

Providing financial assistance to an individual who—

(a) is entitled to—

(i) housing benefit, or

(ii) any other reserved benefit payable in respect of a liability to make rent payments, and

(b) appears to require financial assistance, in addition to any amount the individual receives by way of housing benefit or such other reserved benefit, to meet or help to meet housing costs.

This exception does not except discretionary financial assistance in a reserved benefit.

This exception also does not except providing financial assistance where the requirement for it arises from reduction, non-payability or suspension of a reserved benefit as a result of an individual's conduct (for example, non-compliance with work-related requirements relating to the benefit) unless—

(a) the requirement for it also arises from some exceptional event or exceptional circumstances, and

(b) the requirement for it is immediate.

For the purposes of this exception—

"rent payments"—

(a) has the meaning given from time to time by paragraph 2 of Schedule 1 to the Universal Credit Regulations 2013 (S.I. 2013/376) or any re-enactment of that paragraph, or

(b) if at any time universal credit ceases to be payable to anyone, has the meaning given by that paragraph or any re-enactment of that paragraph immediately before that time;

"reserved benefit" means a benefit which is to any extent a reserved matter."

26 Discretionary payments and assistance

In Section F1 of Part 2 of Schedule 5 to the Scotland Act 1998, in the Exceptions, for the words from "Providing occasional financial" to "unsettled way of life." substitute—

"Exception 7

Providing financial or other assistance to or in respect of individuals who appear to require it for the purposes of meeting, or helping to meet, a short-term need that requires to be met to avoid a risk to the well-being of an individual.

This exception does not except providing assistance where the requirement for it arises from reduction, non-payability or suspension of a benefit as a result of an individual's conduct (for example, non-compliance with work-related requirements relating to the benefit) unless—

(a) the requirement for it also arises from some exceptional event or exceptional circumstances, and

(b) the need is immediate as well as short-term.

Exception 8

Providing occasional financial or other assistance to or in respect of individuals who have been or might otherwise be—

(a) in prison, hospital, a residential care establishment or other institution, or

(b) homeless or otherwise living an unsettled way of life,

and who appear to require the assistance to establish or maintain a settled home."

27 Welfare foods

(1) In Part 2 of Schedule 5 to the Scotland Act 1998, Section F1 is amended as follows.

(2) In the Exceptions, after exception 8 (see section 26 above) insert—

"Exception 9

The subject-matter of section 13 of the Social Security Act 1988 (benefits under schemes for improving nutrition: pregnant women, mothers and children)."

(3) In the Interpretation provision, at the end insert—

"The reference to the subject-matter of section 13 of the Social Security Act 1988 is to be construed as a reference to it as at the day on which section 27 of the Scotland Act 2016 comes into force (and, accordingly, paragraph 5(1) of Part 3 of this Schedule does not apply to that reference)."

(4) Omit Section J5 (welfare foods).

(5) In the Social Security Act 1988, in section 13(2) (benefits under schemes for improving nutrition: consultation) omit "the Scottish Ministers and".

28 Power to create other new benefits

(1) The Scotland Act 1998 is amended as follows.

(2) In Section F1 of Part 2 of Schedule 5, in the Exceptions, after exception 9 (see section 27 above) insert—

"**Exception 10**

Schemes which provide assistance for social security purposes to or in respect of individuals by way of benefits and which—

(a) are supported from sums paid out of the Scottish Consolidated Fund,

(b) do not fall within exceptions 1 to 9, and

(c) are not connected with reserved matters (other than matters reserved only by virtue of this Section).

This exception does not except providing assistance by way of pensions to or in respect of individuals who qualify by reason of old age.

This exception does not except providing assistance where the requirement for it arises from reduction, non-payability or suspension of a reserved benefit as a result of an individual's conduct (for example, non-compliance with work-related requirements relating to the benefit) unless—

(a) the requirement for it also arises from some exceptional event or exceptional circumstances, and

(b) the requirement for it is immediate.

For the purposes of this exception "reserved benefit" means a benefit which is to any extent a reserved matter.

In this exception the reference to schemes supported from sums paid out of the Scottish Consolidated Fund does not include schemes—

(a) in respect of which sums are at some time paid out of the Scottish Consolidated Fund, but

(b) which are directly supported from payments out of the Consolidated Fund, the National Insurance Fund or the Social Fund, or out of money provided by Parliament."

(3) Schedule 4 (enactments etc protected from modification) is amended as follows.

(4) In paragraph 2, at the end insert—

"(5) Sub-paragraph (3) does not affect sub-paragraph (1) as it applies to an Act of the Scottish Parliament so far as any matter to which a provision of the Act relates falls within exception 10 of Section F1 of Part 2 of Schedule 5."

(5) In paragraph 3, at the end insert—

"(3) Sub-paragraph (1) does not affect the application of paragraph 2 to modifications which are incidental to, or consequential on, any provision, if it is only by virtue of exception 10 of Section F1 of Part 2 of Schedule 5 that the provision does not relate to reserved matters."

29 Universal credit: costs of claimants who rent accommodation

(1) A function of making regulations to which this section applies, so far as it is exercisable by the Secretary of State in or as regards Scotland, is exercisable by the Scottish Ministers concurrently with the Secretary of State.

(2) This section applies to—

(a) regulations under section 11(4) of the Welfare Reform Act 2012 (determination and calculation of housing cost element), so far as relating to any liability of a claimant in respect of accommodation which the claimant rents, and

(b) regulations under section 5(1)(p) of the Social Security Administration Act 1992 (payments to another person on behalf of the beneficiary), so far as relating to the payment of an amount of universal credit in respect of any such liability.

(3) For the purposes of this section—

(a) a claimant "rents" accommodation if he or she is liable to make rent payments (with or without other payments) in respect of it, and

(b) "rent payments" has the meaning given from time to time by paragraph 2 of Schedule 1 to the Universal Credit Regulations 2013 (S.I. 2013/376).

(4) The Scottish Ministers may not exercise the function of making regulations to which this section applies unless they have consulted the Secretary of State about the practicability of implementing the regulations.

(5) If—

(a) the Scottish Ministers make regulations to which this section applies, and

(b) the Secretary of State considers that it is not practicable to implement a change made by the regulations by the time that change is to start to have effect,

the Secretary of State may by regulations made by statutory instrument amend the regulations so that the change is to start to have effect from a time later than the time originally set.

(6) The altered time must be no later than the Secretary of State considers necessary, having regard to the practicability of implementing the change.

(7) The Secretary of State may not exercise the function of making regulations to which this section applies in or as regards Scotland unless he or she has consulted the Scottish Ministers.

(8) Where regulations are made by the Scottish Ministers by virtue of subsection (1)—

(a) section 43(1) of the Welfare Reform Act 2012 (in the case of regulations referred to in subsection (2)(a)) and section 189(3) of the Social Security Administration Act 1992 (in the case of regulations referred to in subsection (2)(b)) do not apply, and

(b) the regulations are subject to the negative procedure (see section 28 of the Interpretation and Legislative Reform (Scotland) Act 2010).

30 Universal credit: persons to whom, and time when, paid

(1) A function of making regulations to which this section applies, so far as it is exercisable by the Secretary of State in or as regards Scotland, is exercisable by the Scottish Ministers concurrently with the Secretary of State.

(2) This section applies to regulations under section 5(1)(i) of the Social Security Administration Act 1992, so far as relating to the person to whom, or the time when, universal credit is to be paid.

(3) The Scottish Ministers may not exercise the function of making regulations to which this section applies unless they have consulted the Secretary of State about the practicability of implementing the regulations.

(4) If—

(a) the Scottish Ministers make regulations to which this section applies, and

(b) the Secretary of State considers that it is not practicable to implement a change made by the regulations by the time that change is to start to have effect,

the Secretary of State may by regulations made by statutory instrument amend the regulations so that the change is to start to have effect from a time later than the time originally set.

(5) The altered time must be no later than the Secretary of State considers necessary, having regard to the practicability of implementing the change.

(6) The Secretary of State may not exercise the function of making regulations to which this section applies in or as regards Scotland unless he or she has consulted the Scottish Ministers.

(7) Where regulations are made by the Scottish Ministers by virtue of subsection (1)—

(a) section 189(3) of the Social Security Administration Act 1992 does not apply, and

(b) the regulations are subject to the negative procedure (see section 28 of the Interpretation and Legislative Reform (Scotland) Act 2010).

Employment support

31 Employment support

(1) In Part 2 of Schedule 5 to the Scotland Act 1998, Section H3 (job search and support) is amended as follows.

(2) For the heading "Exception" substitute "Exceptions".

(3) After that heading insert—

"**Exception 1**

The making by a person of arrangements for, or arrangements for the purposes of or in connection with a scheme for, any of the following purposes—

(a) assisting disabled persons to select, obtain and retain employment;

(b) assisting persons claiming reserved benefits who are at risk of long-term unemployment to select, obtain and retain employment, where the assistance is for at least a year;

(c) assisting employers to obtain suitable employees who are persons referred to in paragraph (a) or (b).

The arrangements referred to in this exception include—

(a) securing that the assistance referred to in this exception is provided by another person;

(b) providing or arranging for the provision of facilities, support or services to any person;

(c) the making of payments to any person.

The assistance referred to in this exception includes—

(a) work search support,

(b) skills training, and

(c) work placements for the benefit of the community.

In this exception—

(a) "disabled person" has the same meaning as it has in the Equality Act 2010 as at 28 May 2015 (the date of introduction into Parliament of the Bill for the Scotland Act 2016);

(b) "reserved benefit" means a benefit which is to any extent a reserved matter."

(4) At the beginning of the existing exception which begins "The subject-matter of—" insert—

"**Exception 2**".

(5) The Scotland Act 1998 has effect as if section 56(1)(g) of that Act included a reference to section 17B of the Jobseekers Act 1995.

General

32 Functions exercisable within devolved competence

(1) The Scotland Act 1998 ("the 1998 Act") has effect, in relation to any function so far as exercisable within devolved competence by virtue of a provision of section 22, 23, 24, 25, 26, 27 or 31, as if references to a "pre-commencement enactment" were to—

(a) an Act passed before or in the same session as the relevant date,

(b) any other enactment made before the relevant date,

(c) subordinate legislation under section 106 of the 1998 Act, to the extent that the legislation states that it is to be treated as a pre-commencement enactment,

but did not include the 1998 Act or this Act (or any amendment made by either of those Acts) or, subject to paragraph (c), an enactment comprised in subordinate legislation under either of those Acts.

(2) In this section—

(a) expressions used in the 1998 Act have the same meaning as in that Act;

(b) in relation to a provision of section 22, 23, 24, 25, 26, 27 or 31, the relevant date for any purpose is the date on which the provision comes into force for that purpose.

(3) In section 53 of the 1998 Act (general transfer of functions), after subsection (3) insert—

"(3A) But see sections 9, 32 and 51 of the Scotland Act 2016 (which give "pre-commencement enactment" a different meaning for functions exercisable within devolved competence by virtue of certain provisions of that Act)."

33 Social Security Advisory Committee and Industrial Injuries Advisory Council

(1) Section 53 of the Scotland Act 1998 does not apply in relation to any function of a Minister of the Crown under the legislation relating to social security and industrial injuries advisory bodies.

(2) Section 117 of that Act does not apply in relation to any reference to a Minister of the Crown in that legislation.

(3) In this section—

"the legislation relating to social security and industrial injuries advisory bodies" means any provision of sections 170 to 174 of, and Schedules 5 to 7 to, the Social Security Administration Act 1992 (Social Security Advisory Committee and Industrial Injuries Advisory Council);

"Minister of the Crown" includes the Treasury.

34 Information-sharing

(1) Information held by the Secretary of State for the purpose of a social security function may be supplied by the Secretary of State to the Scottish Ministers for use for the purpose of a relevant Scottish social security function.

(2) Where information is supplied to the Scottish Ministers under subsection (1) for use for any purpose, they may use it for any other purposes for which information held by them for that purpose may be used.

(3) Information held by the Scottish Ministers for the purpose of a relevant Scottish social security function may be supplied by them to the Secretary of State for use for the purpose of a social security function.

(4) Where information is supplied to the Secretary of State under subsection (3) for use for any purpose, the Secretary of State may use it for any other purposes for which information held by him or her for that purpose may be used.

(5) In subsections (1) to (4)—

- (a) references to the Secretary of State include a person providing services to him or her;
- (b) references to the Scottish Ministers include a person providing services to them.

(6) Information supplied under this section must not be supplied by the recipient of the information to any other person or body without—

- (a) the authority of the Secretary of State, in the case of information supplied under subsection (1);
- (b) the authority of the Scottish Ministers, in the case of information supplied under subsection (3).

(7) In this section—

"social security function" means a function of the Secretary of State relating to—

- (a) social security,
- (b) the investigation or prosecution of offences relating to tax credits,
- (c) employment or training,
- (d) war pensions,

(e) welfare foods, or

(f) any other prescribed matter;

"relevant Scottish social security function" means—

(a) a function which is exercisable by the Scottish Ministers within devolved competence by virtue of any of the following provisions of Part 2 of Schedule 5 to the Scotland Act 1998—

(i) exceptions 1, 2, 4 to 8 and 10 in Section F1 (social security schemes), and

(ii) exception 1 in Section H3 (job search and support);

(b) a function of the Scottish Ministers under or by virtue of—

(i) section 29 (universal credit: costs of claimants who rent accommodation), or

(ii) section 30 (universal credit: persons to whom, and time when, paid);

(c) a function of the Scottish Ministers relating to welfare foods;

(d) any other prescribed function of the Scottish Ministers.

(8) In subsection (7)—

(a) the reference to a function being exercisable within devolved competence is to be read in accordance with section 54 of the Scotland Act 1998;

(b) "war pensions" means schemes for the payment of pensions, grants, allowances, supplements or gratuities for or in respect of persons who have a disablement or have died in consequence of service as members of the armed forces of the Crown;

(c) "prescribed" means prescribed by regulations made by the Secretary of State.

(9) Regulations under this section must be made by statutory instrument.

(10) A statutory instrument containing regulations under this section may not be made unless a draft of the instrument has been laid before and approved by a resolution of each House of Parliament.

35 Extension of unauthorised disclosure offence

(1) Part 2 of Schedule 4 to the Social Security Administration Act 1992 is amended as follows.

(2) After paragraph 1A insert—

"1B The reference in Part 1 of this Schedule to the Scottish Administration is a reference to that Administration only to the extent that the functions carried out by persons in its employ—

(a) relate to social security, or

(b) are, or are connected with, functions of the First-tier Tribunal or Upper Tribunal which relate to social security or to occupational or personal pension schemes or to war pensions or functions of the Chief, or any other, Social Security Commissioner."

(3) In paragraph 3, omit ", the Scottish Administration".

PART 4

OTHER LEGISLATIVE COMPETENCE

36 Crown Estate

(1) In Part 5 of the Scotland Act 1998, before the heading "Miscellaneous" insert—

"The Crown Estate

90B The Crown Estate

(1) The Treasury may make a scheme transferring on the transfer date all the existing Scottish functions of the Crown Estate Commissioners ("the Commissioners") to the Scottish Ministers or a person nominated by the Scottish Ministers ("the transferee").

(2) The existing Scottish functions are the Commissioners' functions relating to the part of the Crown Estate that, immediately before the transfer date, consists of—

(a) property, rights or interests in land in Scotland, excluding property, rights or interests mentioned in subsection (3), and

(b) rights in relation to the Scottish zone.

(3) Where immediately before the transfer date part of the Crown Estate consists of property, rights or interests held by a limited partnership registered under the Limited Partnerships Act 1907, subsection (2)(a) excludes—

(a) the property, rights or interests, and

(b) any property, rights or interests in, or in a member of, a partner in the limited partnership.

(4) Functions relating to rights within subsection (2)(b) are to be treated for the purposes of this Act as exercisable in or as regards Scotland.

(5) The property, rights and interests to which the existing Scottish functions relate must continue to be managed on behalf of the Crown.

(6) That does not prevent the disposal of property, rights or interests for the purposes of that management.

(7) Subsection (5) also applies to property, rights or interests acquired in the course of that management (except revenues to which section 1(2) of the Civil List Act 1952 applies).

(8) The property, rights and interests to which subsection (5) applies must be maintained as an estate in land or as estates in land managed separately (with any proportion of cash or investments that seems to the person managing the estate to be required for the discharge of functions relating to its management).

(9) The scheme may specify any property, rights or interests that appear to the Treasury to fall within subsection (2)(a) or (b), without prejudice to the functions transferred by the scheme.

(10) The scheme must provide for the transfer to the transferee of designated rights and liabilities of the Commissioners in connection with the functions transferred.

(11) The scheme must include provision to secure that the employment of any person in Crown employment (within the meaning of section 191 of the Employment Rights Act 1996) is not adversely affected by the transfer.

(12) The scheme must include such provision as the Treasury consider necessary or expedient—

(a) in the interests of defence or national security,

(b) in connection with access to land for the purposes of telecommunications, or with other matters falling within Section C10 in Part 2 of Schedule 5,

(c) for securing that the management of property, rights or interests to which subsection (5) applies does not conflict with the exploitation of resources falling within Section D2 in Part 2 of Schedule 5, or with other reserved matters in connection with their exploitation, and

(d) for securing consistency, in the interests of consumers, in the management of property, rights or interests to which subsection (5) applies and of property, rights or interests to which the Commissioners' functions other than the existing Scottish functions relate, so far as it affects the transmission or distribution of electricity or the provision or use of electricity interconnectors.

(13) Any transfer by the scheme is subject to any provision under subsection (12).

(14) The scheme may include—

(a) incidental, supplemental and transitional provision;

(b) consequential provision, including provision amending an enactment, instrument or other document;

(c) provision conferring or imposing a function on any person including any successor of the transferee;

(d) provision for the creation of new rights or liabilities in relation to the functions transferred.

(15) On the transfer date, the existing Scottish functions and the designated rights and liabilities are transferred and vest in accordance with the scheme.

(16) A certificate by the Treasury that anything specified in the certificate has vested in any person by virtue of the scheme is conclusive evidence for all purposes.

(17) The Treasury may make a scheme under this section only with the agreement of the Scottish Ministers.

(18) The power to make a scheme under this section is exercisable by statutory instrument.

(19) The power to amend the scheme is exercisable so as to provide for an amendment to have effect from the transfer date.

(20) In this section—

"designated" means specified in or determined in accordance with the scheme;

"the transfer date" means a date specified by the scheme as the date on which the scheme is to have effect."

(2) Part 1 of Schedule 5 to the Scotland Act 1998 (general reservations) is amended as follows.

(3) In sub-paragraph (3) of paragraph 2, after "Crown Estate" insert "(that is, the property, rights and interests under the management of the Crown Estate Commissioners)".

(4) After that sub-paragraph insert—

"(3A) Sub-paragraph (1) does not affect the reservation by paragraph 1 of the requirements of section 90B(5) to (8)."

(5) In paragraph 1(2) of Schedule 7 to that Act (procedure for subordinate legislation) in the appropriate place insert—

"Section 90B	Type C"

(6) After paragraph 3 of that Schedule insert—

"3A If legislation under section 90B amends a scheme under that section and does not contain provision—

(a) made by virtue of subsection (12) or (19) of that section, or

(b) adding to, replacing or omitting any part of the text of an Act,

then, instead of the type C procedure, the type I procedure shall apply."

(7) For the purposes of the exercise on and after the transfer date of functions transferred by the scheme under section 90B of the Scotland Act 1998, the Crown Estate Act 1961 applies in relation to the transferee as it applied immediately before that date to the Crown Estate Commissioners, with the following modifications—

(a) a reference to the Crown Estate is to be read as a reference to the property, rights and interests to which section 90B(5) applies;

(b) a reference to the Treasury is to be read as a reference to the Scottish Ministers;

(c) a reference to the Comptroller and Auditor General is to be read as a reference to the Auditor General for Scotland;

(d) a reference to Parliament or either House of Parliament is to be read as a reference to the Scottish Parliament;

(e) the following do not apply—

in section 1, subsections (1), (4) and (7);

in section 2, subsections (1) and (2) and, if the Scottish Ministers are the transferee, the words in subsection (3) from "in relation thereto" to the end;

in section 4, the words "with the consent of Her Majesty signified under the Royal Sign Manual";

sections 5, 7 and 8 and Schedule 1.

(8) Subsection (7) is subject to any provision made by Order in Council under subsection (9) or by any other enactment, including an enactment comprised in, or in an instrument made under, an Act of the Scottish Parliament.

(9) Her Majesty may by Order in Council make such provision as She considers appropriate for or in connection with the exercise by the transferee under the scheme under section 90B of the Scotland Act 1998 (subject to subsections (5) to (8) of that section) of functions transferred by the scheme, including provision taking effect on or before the transfer date.

(10) An Order in Council under subsection (9) may in particular—

(a) establish a body, including a body that may be nominated under that section as the transferee;

(b) amend, repeal, revoke or otherwise modify an enactment, an Act of the Scottish Parliament, or an instrument made under an enactment or Act of the Scottish Parliament.

(11) The power to make an Order in Council under subsection (9) is exercisable by Scottish statutory instrument subject to the affirmative procedure (see section 29 of the Interpretation and Legislative Reform (Scotland) Act 2010).

(12) That power is to be regarded as being exercisable within devolved competence before the transfer date for the purposes of—

(a) section 92(4)(c) of the Scotland Act 1998 (Queen's Printer for Scotland);

(b) section 104(2)(c) of that Act (power to make provision consequential on legislation of, or scrutinised by, the Parliament);

(c) paragraph 11(3)(c) of Schedule 4 to that Act (modification of enactments in relation to making of subordinate legislation).

(13) In section 1(2) of the Civil List Act 1952 (payment of hereditary revenues into the Scottish Consolidated Fund) after "treasure trove" insert "and from the property, rights and interests the management of which is transferred by the scheme under section 90B of the Scotland Act 1998".

(14) In Schedule 1 to the Crown Estate Act 1961, omit paragraph 1(3A) and (4A) (Commissioner with special responsibility for Scotland).

(15) In the Scotland Act 2012, omit section 18.

37 Equal opportunities

(1) Section L2 in Part 2 of Schedule 5 to the Scotland Act 1998 (equal opportunities) is amended as follows.

(2) Omit the words from ", including the subject-matter of" to "1995".

(3) Under the heading "Exceptions", at the end insert—

"Equal opportunities so far as relating to the inclusion of persons with protected characteristics in non-executive posts on boards of Scottish public authorities with mixed functions or no reserved functions.

Equal opportunities in relation to the Scottish functions of any Scottish public authority or cross-border public authority, other than any function that relates to the inclusion of persons in non-executive posts on boards of Scottish public authorities with mixed functions or no reserved functions. The provision falling within this exception does not include any modification of the Equality Act 2010, or of any subordinate legislation made under that Act, but does include—

(a) provision that supplements or is otherwise additional to provision made by that Act;

(b) in particular, provision imposing a requirement to take action that that Act does not prohibit;

(c) provision that reproduces or applies an enactment contained in that Act, with or without modification, without affecting the enactment as it applies for the purposes of that Act."

(4) Under the heading "Interpretation", at the appropriate places insert—

""Board" includes any other equivalent management body."

""Non-executive post" in relation to an authority means any position the holder of which is not an employee of the authority."

""Protected characteristic" has the same meaning as in the Equality Act 2010."

(5) Under that heading, at the end insert—

"The references to the Equality Act 2010 and any subordinate legislation made under that Act are to be read as references to those enactments, as at the day on which section 37 of the Scotland Act 2016 comes into force, but treating any provision of them that is not yet in force on that day as if it were in force."

(6) The Equality Act 2010 is amended as follows.

(7) In section 152(3) (power to specify public authorities: consultation and consent), for the words after "must" substitute "consult the Commission, and after making such an order they must inform a Minister of the Crown."

(8) In the table in section 154(3) (power to impose specific duties: cross-border authorities) in the second column for the words "The Scottish Ministers must consult a Minister of the Crown before" in both places substitute "The Scottish Ministers must inform a Minister of the Crown after".

38 Public sector duty regarding socio-economic inequalities

(1) Part 1 of the Equality Act 2010 (socio-economic inequalities) is amended as follows.

(2) Section 1 (public sector duty) is amended as follows.

(3) In subsection (2) for "by a Minister of the Crown" substitute "in accordance with subsection (2A)".

(4) After subsection (2) insert—

"(2A) The guidance to be taken into account under subsection (2) is—

(a) in the case of a duty imposed on an authority in relation to devolved Scottish functions, guidance issued by the Scottish Ministers;

(b) in any other case, guidance issued by a Minister of the Crown."

(5) Section 2 (power to amend section 1) is amended as follows.

(6) In subsections (7) and (9) omit "the Scottish Ministers or".

(7) In subsection (10) for "the Ministers" substitute "the Welsh Ministers".

(8) In subsection (11) for "section" substitute "Part".

(9) In section 216 of that Act (commencement) at the beginning of subsection (3) insert "Subject to subsection (4)," and after that subsection insert—

"(4) The following provisions of Part 1 (socio-economic inequalities) come into force on such day as the Scottish Ministers may by order appoint—

(a) section 1, so far as it applies to a relevant authority as defined by section 2(5);

(b) section 2, so far as it confers a power on the Scottish Ministers;

(c) section 3, for the purposes of section 1 to the extent mentioned in paragraph (a).

(5) The following do not apply to an order under subsection (4)—

(a) section 207(2) (see instead section 27 of the Interpretation and Legislative Reform (Scotland) Act 2010: powers exercisable by Scottish statutory instrument), and

(b) section 210."

(10) In the Interpretation and Legislative Reform (Scotland) Act 2010, in section 30(4) (other instruments laid before the Parliament: exceptions) after paragraph (i) insert—

"(j) section 216(4) of the Equality Act 2010 (c.15)."

39 Tribunals

(1) In Part 3 of Schedule 5 to the Scotland Act 1998 (reserved matters: general provisions) after paragraph 2 insert—

"2A Tribunals

2A (1) This Schedule does not reserve the transfer to a Scottish tribunal of functions of a tribunal that relate to reserved matters, so far as those functions are exercisable in relation to Scottish cases.

(2) "Scottish cases" has the meaning given by an Order in Council made by Her Majesty under this sub-paragraph.

(3) Sub-paragraph (1) does not apply where a function is excluded from transfer.

(4) Where a function is not excluded from transfer but is subject to qualified transfer, sub-paragraph (1) applies only if the transfer of the function is in accordance with provision made by Her Majesty by Order in Council.

(5) An Order in Council under sub-paragraph (4)—

(a) must specify the function to which it relates,

(b) must specify the Scottish tribunal to which the function may be transferred, and

(c) may make any other provision which Her Majesty considers necessary or expedient for the purposes of or in consequence of the transfer of the function and its exercise by the Scottish tribunal.

(6) The functions that are subject to qualified transfer are the functions of the following tribunals—

(a) the First-tier Tribunal or the Upper Tribunal that are established under section 3 of the Tribunals, Courts and Enforcement Act 2007;

(b) an employment tribunal or the Employment Appeal Tribunal;

(c) a tribunal listed in Schedule 1 to the Tribunals and Inquiries Act 1992;

(d) a tribunal listed in Schedule 6 to the Tribunals, Courts and Enforcement Act 2007.

(7) Sub-paragraph (6)(c) and (d) include a tribunal added to the Schedule concerned after this paragraph comes into force.

(8) Provision made by virtue of sub-paragraph (5)(c) may—

(a) include provision that—

(i) modifies the function;

(ii) imposes conditions or restrictions (including conditions or restrictions relating to the composition or rules of procedure of the Scottish tribunal, or to its staff or accommodation);

(b) be made with a view to purposes including—

(i) securing consistency in any respect in practice or procedure or otherwise between the Scottish tribunal and other tribunals;

(ii) promoting judicial co-operation in the interests of consistency.

(9) Sub-paragraph (8) does not limit the provision that may be made by virtue of sub-paragraph (5)(c).

(10) The following functions are excluded from transfer—

(a) functions of a national security tribunal;

(b) functions of a regulator, or of a person or body that exercises functions on behalf of a regulator;

(c) functions of the Comptroller-General of Patents, Designs and Trade Marks.

(11) In this paragraph—

a "national security tribunal" means—

(a) the Pathogens Access Appeal Commission;

(b) the Proscribed Organisations Appeal Commission;

(c) the Special Immigration Appeals Commission;

(d) the tribunal established by section 65(1) of the Regulation of Investigatory Powers Act 2000 (investigatory powers tribunal);

(e) any other tribunal that has functions relating to matters falling within Section B8 of Part 2 of this Schedule, except a tribunal mentioned in sub-paragraph (6);

a "regulator" means a person or body that has regulatory functions (within the meaning given by section 32 of the Legislative and Regulatory Reform Act 2006);

a "Scottish tribunal" means a tribunal in Scotland—

(a) that does not have functions in or as regards any other country or territory, except for purposes ancillary to its functions in or as regards Scotland, and

(b) that is not, and does not have as a member, a member of the Scottish Government.

(12) The powers conferred by this paragraph do not affect the powers conferred by section 30 or section 113."

(2) In paragraph 1(2) of Schedule 7 to that Act (procedure for subordinate legislation) at the appropriate place insert—

"Schedule 5, Part 3, paragraph 2A	Type A"

(3) Part 1 of Schedule 1 to the Tribunals and Inquiries Act 1992 (tribunals to which the Act applies) is amended as follows.

(4) Before paragraph 9A insert—

"Company names	9ZA. Company names adjudicators appointed under section 70(1) of the Companies Act 2006."

(5) In paragraph 34 (patents, designs and trademarks)—

(a) the words from "the Comptroller-General" to the end become sub-paragraph (a), and

(b) after that sub-paragraph insert—

"(b) a person appointed under section 27A(1)(a) of the Registered Designs Act 1949;

(c) a person appointed under section 77(1) of the Trade Marks Act 1994".

(6) In section 7(2) of the Tribunals and Inquiries Act 1992 (tribunals in relation to which section 7 does not apply) after "3," insert "9ZA,".

(7) In section 14(1)(a) of that Act (restricted application of Act in relation to certain tribunals) after "paragraph" insert "9ZA,".

40 Roads

(1) In Part 2 of Schedule 5 to the Scotland Act 1998, Section E1 (specific reservations: road transport) is amended as follows.

(2) In the reservation relating to the subject-matter of certain enactments, for paragraph (c) (reservation of subject-matter of section 17 and other provisions of the Road Traffic Regulation Act 1984) substitute—

"(c) section 17 of the Road Traffic Regulation Act 1984 (traffic regulation on special roads) except so far as relating to the speed of vehicles on special roads, and section 87 of that Act (exemption of emergency vehicles from speed limits) so far as relating to the training of drivers of vehicles,".

(3) In paragraph (d) of that reservation, after "the Road Traffic Act 1988" insert ", except so far as relating to the parking of vehicles on roads,".

(4) In the first exception relating to the Road Traffic Act 1988, after "sections" insert "36 (offence of failing to comply with traffic sign),".

(5) At the end insert—

"Interpretation

The reference to the subject-matter of section 87 of the Road Traffic Regulation Act 1984 is to be construed as a reference to it as substituted by section 19 of the Road Safety Act 2006 as at the date when section 40 of the Scotland Act 2016 comes into force, treating section 19 and any amendment affecting it at that date as if they were in force (and, accordingly, paragraph 5(1) of Part 3 of this Schedule does not apply to that reference)."

41 Roads: traffic signs etc

(1) The Road Traffic Regulation Act 1984 is amended as follows.

(2) In section 25(1) (Secretary of State to make pedestrian crossing regulations) for "Secretary of State" substitute "national authority".

(3) In section 64 (general provisions as to traffic signs)—

(a) in subsections (1) and (2) for "Secretary of State" substitute "national authority",

(b) in subsection (1) for "Ministers acting jointly" substitute "national authority",

(c) omit subsections (2A) to (2C), and

(d) omit subsections (7) and (8).

(4) Section 65 (powers of traffic authorities as to placing of traffic signs) is amended as follows.

(5) In subsection (1) omit "as may be given by the Ministers acting jointly".

(6) In subsections (1), (2), (3A)(ii) and (4) for "Secretary of State" substitute "national authority".

(7) In subsection (3) after "power" insert "of the Secretary of State".

(8) After that subsection insert—

"(3ZA) The power of the Scottish Ministers to give general directions under subsection (1) is to be exercisable by Scottish statutory instrument.

(3ZB) Before giving a general direction under subsection (1) the Secretary of State must consult with the Scottish Ministers.

(3ZC) Before giving a general direction under subsection (1) the Scottish Ministers must consult with the Secretary of State."

(9) In subsection (3A)(ii) after "prescribed" insert "in regulations made by the national authority".

(10) In section 69(3) (Secretary of State's directions for removal of traffic signs) for "Secretary of State" substitute "national authority".

(11) In section 70(1) (default powers of Secretary of State as to traffic signs)—

(a) for "Secretary of State" substitute "national authority",

(b) omit "himself",

(c) omit "by him" in the first place,

(d) for "him", in the second place, substitute "the national authority", and

(e) after "the authority" insert "that failed to comply with the direction".

(12) In section 71(1) (power to enter land in connection with traffic signs) for "Secretary of State" substitute "national authority".

(13) In section 77 (modification of provisions relating to directions where Secretary of State is the traffic authority) for "Secretary of State", in both places, substitute "national authority".

(14) Section 79 (advances by Secretary of State towards expenses of traffic signs) is amended as follows.

(15) In subsection (1), for the words from "Secretary of State" to "Parliament," substitute "national authority may".

(16) After subsection (1) insert—

"(1A) An advance by the Secretary of State under this section is to be made out of moneys provided by Parliament."

(17) In subsections (3) and (5) for "Secretary of State" substitute "national authority".

(18) In section 142(1) (general interpretation) at the appropriate place insert—

""national authority"—

(a) in relation to a function so far as exercisable within devolved competence, within the meaning of the Scotland Act 1998, means the Scottish Ministers;

(b) otherwise, means the Secretary of State;".

(19) The Road Traffic Act 1988 is amended as follows.

(20) Section 36 (offence of failing to comply with traffic sign) is amended as follows.

(21) In subsections (1)(b) and (3)(a) for "Secretary of State" substitute "national authority".

(22) In subsection (5) for the words from "Secretary of State for the Environment" to "jointly" substitute "national authority".

(23) After subsection (5) insert—

"(6) Before making regulations under subsection (5) the Secretary of State must consult with the Scottish Ministers.

(7) Before making regulations under subsection (5) the Scottish Ministers must consult with the Secretary of State.

(8) In this section "national authority" has the meaning given by section 142(1) of the Road Traffic Regulation Act 1984."

42 Roads: speed limits

(1) The Road Traffic Regulation Act 1984 is amended as follows.

(2) Section 81 (speed limit for restricted roads) is amended as follows.

(3) In subsection (2)—
(a) for "Ministers acting jointly" substitute "national authority", and
(b) omit the words from "made" to "Parliament".

(4) After that subsection insert—

"(3) An order under subsection (2)—
(a) if made by the Secretary of State, is to be made by statutory instrument and approved by a resolution of each House of Parliament;
(b) if made by the Scottish Ministers, is subject to the affirmative procedure.

(4) Before making an order under subsection (2) the Secretary of State must consult with the Scottish Ministers.

(5) Before making an order under subsection (2) the Scottish Ministers must consult with the Secretary of State."

(5) In section 82 (what roads are restricted roads)—
(a) in subsection (1)(b) for "Secretary of State" substitute "Scottish Ministers", and
(b) in subsection (3) for "prescribed manner" substitute "manner prescribed in regulations made by the national authority".

(6) Section 83 (provisions as to directions by a traffic authority under section 82(2)) is amended as follows.

(7) In subsection (1)—
(a) for "Secretary of State", in both places, substitute "national authority", and
(b) for "his" substitute "the national authority's".

(8) Section 84 (speed limits on roads other than restricted roads) is amended as follows.

(9) In subsections (1A) and (1B) for "Secretary of State" substitute "national authority".

(10) Section 85 (traffic signs for indicating speed restrictions) is amended as follows.

(11) In the following places, for "Secretary of State" substitute "national authority"—
(a) subsection (1),
(b) subsection (2)(a) and (b),
(c) subsection (3), and
(d) subsection (5A).

(12) In subsection (1) for "he" substitute "the national authority".

(13) In subsection (3)—
(a) omit "himself",
(b) omit "by him" in the first place, and
(c) for "him", in the second place, substitute "the national authority".

(14) In subsection (5A) omit the words from "or, where" to "officer of the Scottish Ministers".

(15) In subsection (7) after "power" insert "of the Secretary of State".

(16) After subsection (7) insert—

"(8) The power of the Scottish Ministers to give general directions under subsection (2) is to be exercisable by Scottish statutory instrument.

(9) Before giving any general directions under subsection (2) the Secretary of State must consult with the Scottish Ministers.

(10) Before giving any general directions under subsection (2) the Scottish Ministers must consult with the Secretary of State."

(17) In section 87 (exemption of emergency vehicles from speed limits) (as amended by section 19 of the Road Safety Act 2006)—

(a) in paragraph (b) of subsection (1) for "prescribed purposes" substitute "purposes prescribed by regulations made by the national authority",

(b) in that paragraph after "may be" insert "so",

(c) in subsection (2)(a) for "this section" substitute "subsection (3)",

(d) in subsection (4) for "The regulations", in the first place, substitute "Regulations under subsection (3)",

(e) in subsection (5) for "The regulations", in the first place, substitute "Regulations under subsection (3)", and

(f) in subsection (6) for "The regulations" substitute "Regulations under subsection (3)".

43 Roads: parking

(1) The Road Traffic Act 1988 is amended as follows.

(2) Section 20 (parking on verges etc: definition of "heavy commercial vehicle") is amended as follows.

(3) In subsection (5) for "Secretary of State" substitute "national authority".

(4) At the end add—

"(8) In subsection (5) "national authority"—

(a) in relation to a function so far as exercisable within devolved competence, within the meaning of the Scotland Act 1998, means the Scottish Ministers;

(b) otherwise, means the Secretary of State.

(9) Before making any regulations under subsection (5) in relation to vehicles used on roads in Scotland, the Secretary of State must consult the Scottish Ministers."

(5) Section 41 (regulation of construction, weight, equipment and use of vehicles) is amended as follows.

(6) In subsection (1) for "Secretary of State" substitute "national authority".

(7) After subsection (2) insert—

"(2A) In subsection (1) "national authority"—

(a) in relation to a function so far as exercisable within devolved competence, within the meaning of the Scotland Act 1998, means the Scottish Ministers;

(b) otherwise, means the Secretary of State.

(2B) Before making any regulations under this section in relation to the parking of vehicles on roads in Scotland, the Secretary of State must consult the Scottish Ministers."

44 Roads: consequential provision etc

(1) Schedule 2 (roads: consequential and related provision) has effect.

(2) The National Assembly for Wales (Transfer of Functions) Order 1999 (S.I. 1999/672) has effect in relation to the Road Traffic Regulation Act 1984 and the Road Traffic Act 1988 as if the amendments of those Acts by sections 41 and 42(1) to (16) and Schedule 2 were in force immediately before the commencement of the Order.

45 Policing of railways and railway property

(1) In Part 2 of Schedule 5 to the Scotland Act 1998, Section E2 (specific reservations: rail transport) is amended as follows.

(2) Under the heading "Exceptions", after the exception relating to the promotion and construction of railways insert—

"Policing of railways and railway property."

(3) Under the heading "Interpretation", after the definition of "railway" insert—

"“Railway property” has the meaning given by section 75(3) of the Railways and Transport Safety Act 2003."

46 British Transport Police: cross-border public authorities

(1) The following are cross-border public authorities for the purposes of the Scotland Act 1998 ("the 1998 Act")—

(a) the British Transport Police Authority;

(b) the Chief Constable of the British Transport Police Force;

(c) the deputy Chief Constable of the British Transport Police Force;

(d) the assistant Chief Constables of the British Transport Police Force.

(2) In relation to those cross-border public authorities the reference in section 88(3) of the 1998 Act to a pre-commencement enactment is to be read as a reference to the Railways and Transport Safety Act 2003.

(3) Except as provided by subsection (2), the 1998 Act applies in relation to the cross-border public authorities mentioned in subsection (1) in the same way as it applies in relation to cross-border public authorities specified in an Order in Council under section 88(5) of the 1998 Act.

47 Onshore petroleum

(1) Section D2 in Part 2 of Schedule 5 to the Scotland Act 1998 (oil and gas) is amended as follows.

(2) In the Exceptions, before "The manufacture of gas." insert—

> "The granting and regulation of licences to search and bore for and get petroleum that, at the time of the grant of the licence, is within the Scottish onshore area, except for any consideration payable for such licences.
>
> Access to land for the purpose of searching or boring for or getting petroleum under such a licence."

(3) After the Exceptions insert—

> *"Interpretation*
>
> The Scottish onshore area is the area of Scotland that is within the baselines established by any Order in Council under section 1(1)(b) of the Territorial Sea Act 1987 (extension of territorial sea).
>
> "Petroleum" means petroleum within the meaning given by section 1 of the Petroleum Act 1998 in its natural state in strata."

48 Onshore petroleum: consequential amendments

(1) The Petroleum Act 1998 is amended as follows.

(2) Section 3 (licences to search and bore for and get petroleum) is amended as follows.

(3) In subsection (1)—

- (a) for "Secretary of State" substitute "appropriate Minister";
- (b) for "he" substitute "the appropriate Minister".

(4) In subsection (3) for "Secretary of State" in the second place substitute "appropriate Minister".

(5) Section 4 (licences: further provisions) is amended as follows.

(6) In subsection (1) for "Secretary of State" substitute "appropriate Minister".

(7) After that subsection insert—

> "(1A) The Scottish Ministers may not make regulations under subsection (1)(e) prescribing model clauses that may be prescribed under subsection (1B).
>
> (1B) The Secretary of State may make regulations prescribing model clauses on the consideration payable for a licence granted by the Scottish Ministers, and the following so far as they relate to such consideration—
>
> - (a) the measurement of petroleum obtained from the licenced area (including the facilitation of such measurement);
> - (b) the keeping of accounts;
> - (c) cancellation of a licence by the Secretary of State if there has been a failure to pay consideration or to comply with a clause on a matter falling within paragraph (a) or (b).

(1C) Model clauses prescribed under subsection (1B) shall, unless the Secretary of State thinks fit to modify or exclude them in any particular case, be incorporated in any licence granted by the Scottish Ministers."

(8) In subsection (3) for "Any such regulations" substitute "Any regulations made by the Secretary of State".

(9) After that subsection insert—

"(3A) Any regulations made by the Scottish Ministers shall be subject to the negative procedure (see section 28 of the Interpretation and Legislative Reform (Scotland) Act 2010)."

(10) After subsection (4) insert—

"(4A) As soon as practicable after granting a licence under section 3, the Scottish Ministers shall publish notice of the fact in the Edinburgh Gazette stating—

(a) the name of the licensee; and

(b) the situation of the area in respect of which the licence has been granted."

(11) In section 5(9) (existing licences) for "the Secretary of State" in each place substitute "the appropriate Minister".

(12) In section 5A (rights transferred without consent) for "Secretary of State" in each place substitute "appropriate Minister".

(13) In section 5B(1) (information) for "the Secretary of State" in each place substitute "the appropriate Minister".

(14) In section 7 (ancillary rights) in subsection (2)—

(a) at the end of paragraph (b) omit "and", and

(b) at the end of paragraph (c) insert "; and

(d) references to the Secretary of State (or the Minister) in sections 4 and 9 of that Act included references to the Scottish Ministers in relation to licences granted in relation to the Scottish onshore area."

(15) In section 8 (power to inspect plans of mines) for "the Secretary of State" in each place substitute "the appropriate Minister".

(16) After section 8 insert—

"8A Interpretation of Part 1

(1) This section applies for the purposes of this Part.

(2) The "appropriate Minister" means—

(a) in relation to the Scottish onshore area, the Scottish Ministers;

(b) otherwise, the Secretary of State.

(3) The Scottish onshore area is the area of Scotland that is within the baselines established by any Order in Council under section 1(1)(b) of the Territorial Sea Act 1987 (extension of territorial sea).

(4) In subsection (3) "Scotland" has the same meaning as in the Scotland Act 1998."

(17) In section 188(12) of the Energy Act 2004, in the substituted subsection (7A), before paragraph (a) insert—

"(za) Part 1 of the Petroleum Act 1998,".

(18) The Oil Taxation Act 1975 is amended as follows.

(19) In section 12(1A)(a)(ii) (authorities that can revoke licences) after "Secretary of State" insert ", the Scottish Ministers".

(20) In paragraph 1(2) of Schedule 1 (determination of oil fields)—

(a) in paragraph (a) after "granted" insert "by the Secretary of State";

(b) after paragraph (a) insert—

"(aa) is the Scottish Ministers if the area is such that licences can be granted by the Scottish Ministers for all of it under Part 1 of the Petroleum Act 1998;

(ab) is the Secretary of State and the Scottish Ministers acting jointly if the area is such that licences can be granted for part of it by the Secretary of State and for part of it by the Scottish Ministers;".

(21) The Petroleum (Production) (Landward Areas) Regulations 1995 are amended as follows.

(22) In regulation 2 (interpretation) after the entry for "principal licence" insert—

""Scottish onshore area" has the meaning given by section 8A of the Petroleum Act 1998;".

(23) In regulation 3 (application of the regulations) at the beginning of paragraph (1) insert "Subject to paragraph (1A),".

(24) After that paragraph insert—

"(1A) These regulations do not apply to applications for licences to search and bore for, and get, petroleum within the Scottish onshore area."

49 Onshore petroleum: existing licences

(1) The Secretary of State may make any amendment that appears to the Secretary of State to be necessary or expedient in consequence of section 47 or 48—

(a) in any model clause, to the extent that, under Part 1 of the Petroleum Act 1998, it is incorporated, or has effect as if incorporated, in an existing licence, and

(b) in any other provision of an existing licence.

(2) In the case of an existing licence granted in respect of an area ("the licence area") of which part only was within the Scottish onshore area at the time the licence was granted—

(a) the Secretary of State may direct that it is to have effect as a licence in respect of an area comprising that part and a separate licence in respect of an area comprising the rest of the licence area, and

(b) subsection (1) applies in relation to each of those licences as it applies in relation to the existing licence.

(3) The power to make amendments under subsection (1)(a) is exercisable by regulations made by statutory instrument.

(4) A statutory instrument containing regulations under this section is subject to annulment in pursuance of a resolution of either House of Parliament.

(5) In this section "existing licence" means a licence granted, before the commencement of section 47, under—

(a) section 3 of the Petroleum Act 1998, or

(b) section 2 of the Petroleum (Production) Act 1934,

in respect of an area all or part of which is within the Scottish onshore area, within the meaning given by Section D2 of Part 2 of Schedule 5 to the Scotland Act 1998.

50 Consumer advocacy and advice

(1) Part 2 of Schedule 5 to the Scotland Act 1998 (specific reservations) is amended as follows.

(2) In Section C7 (consumer protection)—

(a) for the heading "Exception" substitute "Exceptions";

(b) after that heading insert—

"The provision of consumer advocacy and advice by, or by agreement with, a public body or the holder of a public office."

(3) In Section C8 (product standards, safety and liability) after the heading "Exceptions" insert—

"The provision of consumer advocacy and advice by, or by agreement with, a public body or the holder of a public office."

(4) In Section C9 (weights and measures) after the reservations insert—

"*Exceptions*

The provision of consumer advocacy and advice by, or by agreement with, a public body or the holder of a public office."

(5) In Section C11 (posts)—

(a) for the heading "Exception" substitute "Exceptions";

(b) after that heading insert—

"The provision of consumer advocacy and advice by, or by agreement with, a public body or the holder of a public office, but not any related compulsory levy on postal operators.";

(c) under the heading "Interpretation", before ""postal services"" insert ""postal operator",".

(6) In Section D1 (electricity)—

(a) for the heading "Exception" substitute "Exceptions";

(b) after the exception relating to the Environmental Protection Act 1990 insert—

"The provision of consumer advocacy and advice by, or by agreement with, a public body or the holder of a public office, but not any related compulsory levy on persons supplying, generating, transmitting or distributing electricity."

(7) In Section D2 (oil and gas), at the end of the exceptions insert—

"The provision in relation to gas of consumer advocacy and advice by, or by agreement with, a public body or the holder of a public office, but not any related compulsory levy on persons supplying gas to premises or conveying gas through pipes."

(8) In paragraph 3(2) of Part 3 of Schedule 5 to the Scotland Act 1998 (reserved bodies) at the end insert—

"(e) the Office of Communications,

(f) the Gas and Electricity Markets Authority."

(9) Section 8 of the Utilities Act 2000 (payments by licence holders relating to new arrangements) is amended as follows.

(10) In subsection (2)—

(a) after "payment by the licence holder of sums" insert "— (a)";

(b) at the end insert ", or

(b) relating to such amounts as the Secretary of State considers reasonable in respect of the provision, in or as regards Scotland, of consumer advocacy and advice by, or by agreement with, a public body or the holder of a public office, in relation to gas and electricity consumers".

(11) Omit—

(a) subsection (3A)(bb) and (cb);

(b) in subsection (3A)(f) the words "or Citizens Advice Scotland";

(c) in subsection (3B)(a) the words "(bb)," and ",(cb)";

(d) in subsection (3C) the words "or Citizens Advice Scotland, or by them jointly,".

(12) In subsection (9) after "(3A)" insert "or to amounts mentioned in subsection (2)(b)".

(13) Section 51 of the Postal Services Act 2011 (consumer protection conditions) is amended as follows.

(14) At the end of subsection (2)(c) omit "and" and insert—

"(ca) to make payments relating to such amounts as the Secretary of State considers reasonable in respect of the provision, in or as regards Scotland, of consumer advocacy and advice by, or by agreement with, a public body or the holder of a public office, in relation to users of postal services, and".

(15) In subsection (6) after "(2)(c)" insert ", (ca)".

(16) Omit—

(a) in subsection (2)(c) the words ", Citizens Advice Scotland";

(b) in subsection (4) the words ", Citizens Advice Scotland";

(c) subsection (4)(d), (e) and (f);

(d) in subsection (4A) the words "or Citizens Advice Scotland, or by them jointly,".

51 Functions exercisable within devolved competence: consumer advocacy and advice

(1) The Scotland Act 1998 ("the 1998 Act") has effect, in relation to any function so far as exercisable within devolved competence by virtue of a provision of section 50, as if references to a "pre-commencement enactment" were to—

(a) an Act passed before or in the same session as the relevant date,

(b) any other enactment made before the relevant date,

(c) subordinate legislation under section 106 of the 1998 Act, to the extent that the legislation states that it is to be treated as a pre-commencement enactment,

but did not include the 1998 Act or this Act (or any amendment made by either of those Acts) or, subject to paragraph (c), an enactment comprised in subordinate legislation under either of those Acts.

(2) In this section—

(a) expressions used in the 1998 Act have the same meaning as in that Act;

(b) the relevant date is the date on which section 50 comes into force.

52 Gaming machines on licensed betting premises

(1) In Section B9 in Part 2 of Schedule 5 to the Scotland Act 1998 (betting, gaming and lotteries) at the end insert—

"*Exception*

In the case of a betting premises licence under the Gambling Act 2005, other than one in respect of a track, the number of gaming machines authorised for which the maximum charge for use is more than £10 (or whether such machines are authorised)."

(2) Section 172 of the Gambling Act 2005 (gaming machines) is amended as follows.

(3) In subsection (11) for "Secretary of State" substitute "appropriate Minister".

(4) After that subsection insert—

"(12) In subsection (11) "the appropriate Minister" means—

(a) the Scottish Ministers, so far as, in the case of a betting premises licence in respect of premises in Scotland and not in respect of a track, the order varies—

(i) the number of gaming machines authorised for which the maximum charge for use is more than £10, or

(ii) whether such machines are authorised;

(b) otherwise, the Secretary of State."

(5) In section 355 of that Act (regulations, orders and rules)—

(a) in subsection (1) after "the Secretary of State" insert "or the Scottish Ministers", and

(b) for subsections (9) and (10) substitute—

"(9) Subsection (3) does not apply to regulations made by the Scottish Ministers (see section 27 of the Interpretation and Legislative Reform (Scotland) Act 2010: functions exercisable by Scottish statutory instrument).

(10) Regulations made by the Scottish Ministers under a provision specified in subsection (4), or under section 285, and an order made by the Scottish Ministers under section 172, shall be subject to the affirmative procedure.

(11) Any other regulations made by the Scottish Ministers under a provision of this Act shall be subject to the negative procedure."

(6) The amendments made by this section do not apply in relation to a betting premises licence issued before this section comes into force.

53 Abortion

In Part 2 of Schedule 5 to the Scotland Act 1998 (specific reservations) omit Section J1 (abortion).

PART 5

OTHER EXECUTIVE COMPETENCE

54 Gaelic Media Service

(1) In section 183A of the Broadcasting Act 1990 (membership of the Gaelic Media Service)—

(a) in subsection (4) for "the Secretary of State and the Scottish Ministers" substitute "the Scottish Ministers", and

(b) in subsection (6)(b) for "the Secretary of State with the agreement of the Scottish Ministers" substitute "the Scottish Ministers".

(2) Section 17(4) to (6) of the Scotland Act 2012 is repealed.

55 Commissioners of Northern Lighthouses

(1) Schedule 8 to the Merchant Shipping Act 1995 (Commissioners of Northern Lighthouses) is amended as follows.

(2) In paragraph 1(2) (the Commissioners), after paragraph (e) insert—

"(f) a person appointed by the Secretary of State (in addition to the person nominated under paragraph (d));

(g) a person appointed by the Scottish Ministers."

(3) In paragraph 2(2) (elections by the Commissioners) for "five" substitute "three".

(4) After paragraph 4 insert—

"4A (1) The Commissioners shall send to the Scottish Ministers a copy of any accounts that they have been required to provide under section 218.

(2) The Scottish Ministers shall lay those accounts before the Scottish Parliament.

(3) The Commissioners shall send to the Scottish Ministers any report made under section 198(4)(b) (reports on inspections).

(4) The Scottish Ministers shall lay any such report before the Scottish Parliament."

56 Maritime and Coastguard Agency

(1) In section 1 of the Coastguard Act 1925 (transfer of the coastguard to the Board of Trade), at the end insert—

"(3) The Secretary of State must consult the Scottish Ministers about the strategic priorities of the Secretary of State in exercising functions under subsection (1) in relation to activities of Her Majesty's Coastguard in Scotland.

(4) In subsection (3) "Scotland" has the same meaning as in the Scotland Act 1998."

(2) In section 292 of the Merchant Shipping Act 1995 (general functions of the Secretary of State) after subsection (2) insert—

"(3) The Secretary of State must consult the Scottish Ministers about the strategic priorities of the Secretary of State in exercising functions under subsection (1) in relation to the safety standards of ships in Scotland and protecting the health and safety of persons on them.

(4) In subsection (3) "Scotland" has the same meaning as in the Scotland Act 1998."

57 Rail: franchising of passenger services

(1) Section 25 of the Railways Act 1993 (public sector operators not to be franchisees) is amended as follows.

(2) In the heading, at the beginning insert "England and Wales:".

(3) After subsection (2) insert—

"(2A) Subsection (1) does not prevent a public sector operator from being a franchisee in relation to a Scottish franchise agreement."

(4) This section does not have effect in relation to any invitation to tender under section 26(2) of the Railways Act 1993 issued before the day on which this section comes into force.

58 Fuel poverty: support schemes

(1) The Energy Act 2010 is amended as follows.

(2) In section 9 (schemes for reducing fuel poverty) after subsection (1) insert—

"(1A) In relation to Scotland, that is subject to section 14A (power of the Scottish Ministers to make schemes)."

(3) After section 14 (regulations under Part 2: procedure) insert—

"14A Power of the Scottish Ministers to make schemes under Part 2

(1) Subject to the following provisions of this section the power under section 9 to make a scheme in relation to Scotland is exercisable by the Secretary of State so as to make only—

(a) provision as to the licensed suppliers to whom the scheme applies,

(b) provision as to the aggregate amount of benefits to be provided under it by scheme suppliers, and

(c) any other provision within section 9(4) or (9)(a) or (c)(v) or (vi).

(2) The power to make other provision under that section for the purposes of the scheme is exercisable by the Scottish Ministers.

(3) For the purposes of the exercise of that power by the Scottish Ministers, this Part applies—

(a) as if references to the Secretary of State in sections 9, 10 and 14(1) and (4) were references to the Scottish Ministers;

(b) as if in section 10(7) "Parliament" were "the Scottish Parliament".

(4) The power of the Scottish Ministers under section 9 does not include power to make provision in relation to the subject-matter of sections 88 to 90 of the Energy Act 2008 (smart meters).

(5) The Scottish Ministers may not make regulations under section 9 unless—

(a) they have consulted the Secretary of State about the proposed regulations, and

(b) the Secretary of State has agreed to the regulations being made.

(6) Subsections (1) and (2) do not prevent the Secretary of State from making any provision under section 9 for the purposes of a scheme in relation to Scotland, or from varying or revoking regulations made by the Scottish Ministers under that section,—

(a) with the agreement of the Scottish Ministers, or

(b) without their agreement, if subsection (7), (9) or (11) applies.

(7) This subsection applies if—

(a) a scheme in relation to England and Wales has been made, or the Secretary of State intends to make such a scheme, and

(b) the Secretary of State is satisfied, after consulting the Scottish Ministers, that, to ensure that a scheme in relation to Scotland is made with a corresponding scheme period, it is necessary for the Secretary of State to make any provision not mentioned in subsection (1)(a) to (c).

(8) In paragraph (b) of subsection (7) a "corresponding scheme period" means a scheme period beginning and ending at the same time as that specified or to be specified in the scheme mentioned in paragraph (a).

(9) This subsection applies if it appears to the Secretary of State that a support scheme made in relation to Scotland is, alone or in conjunction with a scheme made or to be made in relation to England and Wales, likely to—

(a) cause detriment to the United Kingdom, or

(b) adversely affect the ability of the United Kingdom to comply with an international agreement or arrangement in relation to climate change or energy efficiency,

and the Scottish Ministers have failed to comply with a request made to them by the Secretary of State to make modifications specified by the Secretary of State.

(10) In determining for the purposes of subsection (9) whether detriment is likely to be caused to the United Kingdom, considerations that the Secretary of State may take into account include the costs imposed on suppliers by virtue of schemes made, or to be made, by the Secretary of State and the Scottish Ministers under section 9.

(11) This subsection applies if—

(a) the Secretary of State makes or intends to make changes to a support scheme which would result in a significant change in the costs incurred by suppliers in complying with the scheme, and

(b) the Scottish Ministers have failed to comply with a request made to them by the Secretary of State to make modifications specified by the Secretary of State.

(12) A request by the Secretary of State to the Scottish Ministers for the purposes of subsection (9) or (11)—

(a) must be in writing;

(b) must specify only modifications that appear to the Secretary of State to be necessary to prevent the effect mentioned in subsection (9)(a) or (b), or (as the case may be) to be necessary or expedient in view of the effect mentioned in subsection (11)(a);

(c) must specify the time within which the modifications are to be made, which must not be less than 2 months from the date of the request.

(13) Section 14(5) does not apply to regulations by which the Secretary of State makes provision by virtue of subsection (6), with or without other provision under section 9."

(4) Section 31 (orders and regulations) is amended as follows.

(5) After subsection (1) insert—

"(1A) Subsection (1) does not apply to regulations made by the Scottish Ministers (see section 27 of the Interpretation and Legislative Reform (Scotland) Act 2010: functions exercisable by Scottish statutory instrument)."

(6) After subsection (4) insert—

"(4A) Regulations made by the Scottish Ministers under section 9 are subject to the affirmative procedure (see section 29 of the Interpretative and Legislative Reform (Scotland) Act 2010)."

(7) In subsection (6) after "Regulations" insert "made by the Secretary of State".

(8) After subsection (6) insert—

"(6A) Regulations made by the Scottish Ministers may impose obligations or confer functions on a person (including the Scottish Ministers)."

(9) Where an amendment made by this section imposes a requirement to consult or to obtain consent, the requirement may be satisfied by consultation undertaken or consent obtained before this section comes into force.

59 Energy company obligations

(1) The Gas Act 1986 is amended as follows.

(2) After section 33BC (promotion of reduction in carbon emissions) insert—

"33BCA Scottish Ministers' promotion of reductions in carbon emissions: gas suppliers

(1) Where the Secretary of State under section 33BC imposes on gas suppliers obligations to achieve a target within a specified period, the power to make orders under that section is exercisable by the Scottish Ministers for the purposes of those obligations imposed in relation to Scotland and not, except as provided by subsections (9) and (10), by the Secretary of State.

(2) An obligation is imposed in relation to Scotland to the extent that measures to meet that obligation may be carried out in Scotland (disregarding any power to elect under section 103 of the Utilities Act 2000).

(3) For the purposes of the exercise by the Scottish Ministers of the power to make an order under section 33BC, that section applies with the following modifications—

(a) for subsection (1) there is substituted a power by order to specify how gas suppliers may meet their obligations to achieve the carbon emissions reduction target through measures carried out in Scotland;

(b) subsections (1A), (3), (5)(a), (7)(a) and (10A) are omitted;

(c) in subsection (2A) at the beginning of paragraph (b) there is inserted "where the Secretary of State has apportioned the overall carbon emissions reduction target under section 103(2A) of the Utilities Act 2000, and";

(d) in subsection (11) "Citizens Advice" and "gas transporters" are omitted;

(e) in subsection (12), for the words from "shall not be made" to the end is substituted "is subject to the affirmative procedure";

(f) in subsection (12A) for the words from "shall be subject to" to the end is substituted "is subject to the negative procedure";

(g) for "Secretary of State" in each place is substituted "Scottish Ministers".

(4) The power of the Scottish Ministers under section 33BC does not include power to make provision in relation to the subject-matter of sections 88 to 90 of the Energy Act 2008 (smart meters).

(5) Where an overall carbon emissions reduction target has been apportioned under section 103(2A) of the Utilities Act 2000, the Scottish Ministers must—

(a) when making any order under section 33BC, comply with the duty in subsection (6), and

(b) if the Secretary of State amends any order under that section, make any provision they think necessary, in consequence of the amendment, to comply with that duty.

(6) The duty of the Scottish Ministers where subsection (5)(a) or (b) applies is to exercise their powers under section 33BC (subject to subsection (8)) in the way they think most likely to secure that the proportion of compliance costs that is represented by costs relating to Scotland is no greater than the proportion of the overall carbon emissions reduction target that is represented by the part of it apportioned to measures carried out in Scotland.

(7) In subsection (6)—

(a) "compliance costs" means the total costs to gas suppliers of complying with carbon emissions reduction obligations that, in relation to any period, are imposed by order under section 33BC, and

(b) "costs relating to Scotland" means the total costs to gas suppliers of complying with obligations that, in relation to the same period, are imposed in relation to Scotland.

(8) The Scottish Ministers may not make an order under section 33BC unless—

(a) they have consulted the Secretary of State about the proposed order, and

(b) the Secretary of State has agreed to the order being made.

(9) Subsection (1) does not prevent the Secretary of State from making provision under—

(a) section 33BC(1A), (3), (5)(a) or (7)(a), or

(b) section 33BC(2A) where an overall carbon emissions reduction target has not been apportioned under section 103(2A) of the Utilities Act 2000.

(10) Subsection (1) does not prevent the Secretary of State from making any other provision under section 33BC or from varying or revoking an order made by the Scottish Ministers under that section—

(a) with the agreement of the Scottish Ministers, or

(b) without their agreement, if subsection (11) applies.

(11) This subsection applies if it appears to the Secretary of State, in the case of obligations imposed in relation to Scotland (the "Scottish obligations"), taking into account any provision made by the Scottish Ministers, that the Scottish obligations are, alone or in conjunction with obligations imposed or to be imposed in relation to England and Wales, likely to—

(a) cause detriment to the United Kingdom,

(b) adversely affect the ability of the United Kingdom to comply with an international agreement or arrangement in relation to climate change or energy efficiency, or

(c) result in costs incurred by suppliers that are not broadly equivalent in relation to England and Wales and in relation to Scotland,

and the Scottish Ministers have failed to comply with a request made to them by the Secretary of State to make modifications specified by the Secretary of State.

(12) In determining for the purposes of subsection (11), whether detriment is likely to be caused to the United Kingdom, considerations that the Secretary of State may take into account include the costs imposed on suppliers by virtue of obligations imposed or to be imposed by the Secretary of State under section 33BC or any provision made by the Scottish Ministers under that section.

(13) A request by the Secretary of State to the Scottish Ministers for the purposes of subsection (11)—

(a) must be in writing;

(b) must specify only modifications that appear to the Secretary of State to be necessary to prevent the effect mentioned in subsection (11)(a), (b) or (c);

(c) must specify the time within which the modifications are to be made, which must not be less than 2 months from the date of the request."

(3) After section 33BD (promotion of reductions in home-heating costs) insert—

"33BDA Scottish Ministers' promotion of reductions in home-heating costs: gas suppliers

(1) Where the Secretary of State under section 33BD imposes on gas suppliers obligations to achieve a target within a specified period, the power to make orders under that section is exercisable by the Scottish Ministers for the purposes of those obligations imposed in relation to Scotland and not, except as provided by subsections (9) and (10), by the Secretary of State.

(2) An obligation is imposed in relation to Scotland to the extent that measures to meet that obligation may be carried out in Scotland (disregarding any power to elect under section 103A of the Utilities Act 2000).

(3) For the purposes of the exercise by the Scottish Ministers of the power to make an order under section 33BD, that section applies with the following modifications—

(a) for subsection (1) there is substituted a power by order to specify how gas suppliers may meet their obligations to achieve the home-heating cost reduction target through measures carried out in Scotland;

(b) subsection (3) is omitted;

(c) subsections (3), (5)(a), (7)(a) and (10A) of section 33BC as applied by subsection (4) are omitted;

(d) in subsection (2)(a) at the beginning of sub-paragraph (ii) there is inserted "where the Secretary of State has apportioned the overall home-heating cost reduction target under section 103A(3A) of the Utilities Act 2000, and";

(e) in section 33BC(11) as applied by subsection (4) "Citizens Advice" and "gas transporters" are omitted;

(f) in section 33BC(12) as applied by subsection (4) for the words from "shall not be made" to the end is substituted "is subject to the affirmative procedure";

(g) in section 33BC(12A) as applied by subsection (4) for the words from "shall be subject to" to the end is substituted "is subject to the negative procedure";

(h) for "Secretary of State" in each place (including any references in section 33BC that apply by virtue of subsection (4)), is substituted "Scottish Ministers".

(4) The power of the Scottish Ministers under section 33BD does not include power to make provision in relation to the subject-matter of sections 88 to 90 of the Energy Act 2008 (smart meters).

(5) Where an overall home-heating cost reduction target has been apportioned under section 103A(3A) of the Utilities Act 2000, the Scottish Ministers must—

(a) when making any order under section 33BD, comply with the duty in subsection (6), and

(b) if the Secretary of State amends any order under that section, make any provision they think necessary, in consequence of the amendment, to comply with that duty.

(6) The duty of the Scottish Ministers where subsection (5)(a) or (b) applies is to exercise their powers under section 33BD (subject to subsection (8)) in the way they think most likely to secure that the proportion of compliance costs that is represented by costs relating to Scotland is no greater than the proportion of the overall home-heating cost reduction target that is represented by the part of it apportioned to measures carried out in Scotland.

(7) In subsection (6)—

(a) "compliance costs" means the total costs to gas suppliers of complying with home-heating cost reduction obligations that, in relation to any period, are imposed by order under section 33BD, and

(b) "costs relating to Scotland" means the total costs to gas suppliers of complying with obligations that, in relation to the same period, are imposed in relation to Scotland.

(8) The Scottish Ministers may not make an order under section 33BD unless—

(a) they have consulted the Secretary of State about the proposed order, and

(b) the Secretary of State has agreed to the order being made.

(9) Subsection (1) does not prevent the Secretary of State from making provision under—

(a) section 33BD(3),

(b) section 33BC(3), (5)(a) or (7)(a) as applied by section 33BD(4), or

(c) section 33BD(2)(a) where an overall home-heating cost reduction target has not been apportioned under section 103A(3A) of the Utilities Act 2000.

(10) Subsection (1) does not prevent the Secretary of State from making any other provision under section 33BD or from varying or revoking an order made by the Scottish Ministers under that section—

(a) with the agreement of the Scottish Ministers, or

(b) without their agreement, if subsection (11) applies.

(11) This subsection applies if it appears to the Secretary of State, in the case of obligations imposed in relation to Scotland (the "Scottish obligations"), taking

into account any provision made by the Scottish Ministers, that the Scottish obligations are, alone or in conjunction with obligations imposed or to be imposed in relation to England and Wales, likely to—

(a) cause detriment to the United Kingdom,

(b) adversely affect the ability of the United Kingdom to comply with an international agreement or arrangement in relation to climate change or energy efficiency, or

(c) result in costs incurred by suppliers that are not broadly equivalent in relation to England and Wales and in relation to Scotland,

and the Scottish Ministers have failed to comply with a request made to them by the Secretary of State to make modifications specified by the Secretary of State.

(12) In determining for the purposes of subsection (11), whether detriment is likely to be caused to the United Kingdom, considerations that the Secretary of State may take into account include the costs imposed on suppliers by virtue of obligations imposed or to be imposed by the Secretary of State under section 33BD or any provision made by the Scottish Ministers under that section.

(13) A request by the Secretary of State to the Scottish Ministers for the purposes of subsection (11)—

(a) must be in writing;

(b) must specify only modifications that appear to the Secretary of State to be necessary to prevent the effect mentioned in subsection (11)(a), (b) or (c);

(c) must specify the time within which the modifications are to be made, which must not be less than 2 months from the date of the request."

(4) The Electricity Act 1989 is amended as follows.

(5) After section 41A (promotion of reductions in carbon emissions) insert—

"41AA Scottish Ministers' promotion of reductions in carbon emissions: electricity suppliers

(1) Where the Secretary of State under section 41A imposes on electricity suppliers obligations to achieve a target within a specified period, the power to make orders under that section is exercisable by the Scottish Ministers for the purposes of those obligations imposed in relation to Scotland and not, except as provided by subsections (9) and (10), by the Secretary of State.

(2) An obligation is imposed in relation to Scotland to the extent that measures to meet that obligation may be carried out in Scotland (disregarding any power to elect under section 103 of the Utilities Act 2000).

(3) For the purposes of the exercise by the Scottish Ministers of the power to make an order under section 41A, that section applies with the following modifications—

(a) for subsection (1) there is substituted a power by order to specify how electricity suppliers may meet their obligations to achieve the carbon emissions reduction target through measures carried out in Scotland;

(b) subsections (1A), (3), (5)(a), (7)(a) and (10A) are omitted;

(c) in subsection (2A) at the beginning of paragraph (b) there is inserted "where the Secretary of State has apportioned the overall carbon emissions reduction target under section 103(2A) of the Utilities Act 2000, and";

(d) in subsection (11) "Citizens Advice" and "electricity distributors" are omitted;

(e) in subsection (12), for the words from "shall not be made" to the end is substituted "is subject to the affirmative procedure";

(f) in subsection (12A) for the words from "shall be subject to" to the end is substituted "is subject to the negative procedure";

(g) for "Secretary of State" in each place is substituted "Scottish Ministers".

(4) The power of the Scottish Ministers under section 41A does not include power to make provision in relation to the subject-matter of sections 88 to 90 of the Energy Act 2008 (smart meters).

(5) Where an overall carbon emissions reduction target has been apportioned under section 103(2A) of the Utilities Act 2000, the Scottish Ministers must—

(a) when making any order under section 41A, comply with the duty in subsection (6), and

(b) if the Secretary of State amends any order under that section, make any provision they think necessary, in consequence of the amendment, to comply with that duty.

(6) The duty of the Scottish Ministers where subsection (5)(a) or (b) applies is to exercise their powers under section 41A (subject to subsection (8)) in the way they think most likely to secure that the proportion of compliance costs that is represented by costs relating to Scotland is no greater than the proportion of the overall carbon emissions reduction target that is represented by the part of it apportioned to measures carried out in Scotland.

(7) In subsection (6)—

(a) "compliance costs" means the total costs to electricity suppliers of complying with carbon emissions reduction obligations that, in relation to any period, are imposed by order under section 41A, and

(b) "costs relating to Scotland" means the total costs to electricity suppliers of complying with obligations that, in relation to the same period, are imposed in relation to Scotland.

(8) The Scottish Ministers may not make an order under section 41A unless—

(a) they have consulted the Secretary of State about the proposed order, and

(b) the Secretary of State has agreed to the order being made.

(9) Subsection (1) does not prevent the Secretary of State from making provision under—

(a) section 41A(1A), (3), (5)(a) or (7)(a), or

(b) section 41A(2A) where an overall carbon emissions reduction target has not been apportioned under section 103(2A) of the Utilities Act 2000.

(10) Subsection (1) does not prevent the Secretary of State from making any other provision under section 41A or from varying or revoking an order made by the Scottish Ministers under that section—

(a) with the agreement of the Scottish Ministers, or

(b) without their agreement, if subsection (11) applies.

(11) This subsection applies if it appears to the Secretary of State, in the case of obligations imposed in relation to Scotland (the "Scottish obligations"), taking into account any provision made by the Scottish Ministers, that the Scottish obligations are, alone or in conjunction with obligations imposed or to be imposed in relation to England and Wales, likely to—

(a) cause detriment to the United Kingdom,

(b) adversely affect the ability of the United Kingdom to comply with an international agreement or arrangement in relation to climate change or energy efficiency, or

(c) result in costs incurred by suppliers that are not broadly equivalent in relation to England and Wales and in relation to Scotland,

and the Scottish Ministers have failed to comply with a request made to them by the Secretary of State to make modifications specified by the Secretary of State.

(12) In determining for the purposes of subsection (11), whether detriment is likely to be caused to the United Kingdom, considerations that the Secretary of State may take into account include the costs imposed on suppliers by virtue of obligations imposed or to be imposed by the Secretary of State under section 41A or any provision made by the Scottish Ministers under that section.

(13) A request by the Secretary of State to the Scottish Ministers for the purposes of subsection (11)—

(a) must be in writing;

(b) must specify only modifications that appear to the Secretary of State to be necessary to prevent the effect mentioned in subsection (11)(a), (b) or (c);

(c) must specify the time within which the modifications are to be made, which must not be less than 2 months from the date of the request."

(6) After section 41B (promotion of reductions in home-heating costs) insert—

"41BA Scottish Ministers' promotion of reductions in home-heating costs: electricity suppliers

(1) Where the Secretary of State under section 41B imposes on electricity suppliers obligations to achieve a target within a specified period, the power to make orders under that section is exercisable by the Scottish Ministers for the purposes of those obligations imposed in relation to Scotland and not, except as provided by subsections (9) and (10), by the Secretary of State.

(2) An obligation is imposed in relation to Scotland to the extent that measures to meet that obligation may be carried out in Scotland (disregarding any power to elect under section 103A of the Utilities Act 2000).

(3) For the purposes of the exercise by the Scottish Ministers of the power to make an order under section 41B, that section applies with the following modifications—

(a) for subsection (1) there is substituted a power by order to specify how electricity suppliers may meet their obligations to achieve the home-heating cost reduction target through measures carried out in Scotland;

(b) subsection (3) is omitted;

(c) subsections (3), (5)(a), (7)(a) and (10A) of section 41A as applied by subsection (4) are omitted;

(d) in subsection (2)(a) at the beginning of sub-paragraph (ii) there is inserted "where the Secretary of State has apportioned the overall home-heating costs reduction target under section 103A(3A) of the Utilities Act 2000, and";

(e) in section 41A(11) as applied by subsection (4) "Citizens Advice" and "electricity distributors" are omitted;

(f) in section 41A(12) as applied by subsection (4) for the words from "shall not be made" to the end is substituted "is subject to the affirmative procedure";

(g) in section 41A(12A) as applied by subsection (4) for the words from "shall be subject to" to the end is substituted "is subject to the negative procedure";

(h) for "Secretary of State" in each place (including any references in section 41A that apply by virtue of subsection (4)), is substituted "Scottish Ministers".

(4) The power of the Scottish Ministers under section 41B does not include power to make provision in relation to the subject-matter of sections 88 to 90 of the Energy Act 2008 (smart meters).

(5) Where an overall home-heating cost reduction target has been apportioned under section 103A(3A) of the Utilities Act 2000, the Scottish Ministers must—

(a) when making any order under section 41B, comply with the duty in subsection (6), and

(b) if the Secretary of State amends any order under that section, make any provision they think necessary, in consequence of the amendment, to comply with that duty.

(6) The duty of the Scottish Ministers where subsection (5)(a) or (b) applies is to exercise their powers under section 41B (subject to subsection (8)) in the way they think most likely to secure that the proportion of compliance costs that is represented by costs relating to Scotland is no greater than the proportion of the overall home-heating cost reduction target that is represented by the part of it apportioned to measures carried out in Scotland.

(7) In subsection (6)—

(a) "compliance costs" means the total costs to electricity suppliers of complying with home-heating cost reduction obligations that, in relation to any period, are imposed by order under section 41B, and

(b) "costs relating to Scotland" means the total costs to electricity suppliers of complying with obligations that, in relation to the same period, are imposed in relation to Scotland.

(8) The Scottish Ministers may not make an order under section 41B unless—

(a) they have consulted the Secretary of State about the proposed order, and

(b) the Secretary of State has agreed to the order being made.

(9) Subsection (1) does not prevent the Secretary of State from making provision under—

(a) section 41B(3),

(b) section 41A(3), (5)(a) or (7)(a) as applied by section 41B(4), or

(c) section 41B(2)(a) where an overall home-heating cost reduction target has not been apportioned under section 103A(3A) of the Utilities Act 2000.

(10) Subsection (1) does not prevent the Secretary of State from making any other provision under section 41B or from varying or revoking an order made by the Scottish Ministers under that section—

(a) with the agreement of the Scottish Ministers, or

(b) without their agreement, if subsection (11) applies.

(11) This subsection applies if it appears to the Secretary of State, in the case of obligations imposed in relation to Scotland (the "Scottish obligations"), taking into account any provision made by the Scottish Ministers, that the Scottish obligations are, alone or in conjunction with obligations imposed or to be imposed in relation to England and Wales, likely to—

(a) cause detriment to the United Kingdom,

(b) adversely affect the ability of the United Kingdom to comply with an international agreement or arrangement in relation to climate change or energy efficiency, or

(c) result in costs incurred by suppliers that are not broadly equivalent in relation to England and Wales and in relation to Scotland,

and the Scottish Ministers have failed to comply with a request made to them by the Secretary of State to make modifications specified by the Secretary of State.

(12) In determining for the purposes of subsection (11), whether detriment is likely to be caused to the United Kingdom, considerations that the Secretary of State may take into account include the costs imposed on suppliers by virtue of obligations imposed or to be imposed by the Secretary of State under section 41B or any provision made by the Scottish Ministers under that section.

(13) A request by the Secretary of State to the Scottish Ministers for the purposes of subsection (11)—

(a) must be in writing;

(b) must specify only modifications that appear to the Secretary of State to be necessary to prevent the effect mentioned in subsection (11)(a), (b) or (c);

(c) must specify the time within which the modifications are to be made, which must not be less than 2 months from the date of the request."

(7) Where an amendment made by this section imposes a requirement to consult or to obtain consent, the requirement may be satisfied by consultation undertaken or consent obtained before this section comes into force.

60 Apportionment of targets

(1) The Utilities Act 2000 is amended as follows.

(2) Section 103 (overall carbon emissions reduction targets) is amended as follows.

(3) After subsection (2) insert—

"(2A) Where an overall target applies in relation to a section mentioned in subsection (1) the order specifying the target may make provision for the target to be apportioned between—

(a) measures carried out in England and Wales, and

(b) measures carried out in Scotland,

by reference to such criteria as may be specified in the order."

(4) After subsection (3) insert—

"(3A) Where a target is apportioned under subsection (2A) for the purposes of a section, an order under that section may include provision for a supplier to elect, subject to any conditions specified in the order—

(a) that, for the purposes of meeting the carbon emissions reduction target under an obligation imposed by the order in relation to England and Wales, a measure carried out in Scotland is to be treated instead as carried out in England and Wales;

(b) that, for the purposes of meeting the carbon emissions reduction target under an obligation imposed by the order in relation to Scotland, a measure carried out in England and Wales is to be treated instead as carried out in Scotland.

(3B) An order may not make provision under subsection (3A)(b) unless the Scottish Ministers have agreed to such provision being made."

(5) Section 103A (overall home-heating cost reduction targets) is amended as follows.

(6) After subsection (3) insert—

"(3A) Where an overall target applies in relation to a section mentioned in subsection (1) the order specifying the target may make provision for the target to be apportioned between—

(a) measures carried out in England and Wales, and

(b) measures carried out in Scotland,

by reference to such criteria as may be specified in the order."

(7) After subsection (4) insert—

"(4A) Where a target is apportioned under subsection (3A) for the purposes of a section, an order under that section may include provision for a supplier to elect, subject to any conditions specified in the order,—

(a) that, for the purposes of meeting the home-heating cost reduction target under an obligation imposed by the order in relation to England and Wales, a measure carried out in Scotland is to be treated instead as carried out in England and Wales;

(b) that, for the purposes of meeting the home-heating cost reduction target under an obligation imposed by the order in relation to Scotland, a measure carried out in England and Wales is to be treated instead as carried out in Scotland.

(4B) An order may not make provision under subsection (4A)(b) unless the Scottish Ministers have agreed to such provision being made."

(8) Section 103B (power to require information) is amended as follows.

(9) In the heading after "Secretary of State" insert "and the Scottish Ministers".

(10) In subsection (1) at the beginning insert "Subject to subsection (1A)," and after that subsection insert—

"(1A) The Scottish Ministers may exercise the power in subsection (1)(b) and (c) in order to require information to review the operation of any carbon emissions reduction order or home-heating cost reduction order made by the Scottish Ministers and to establish and maintain a measures record in relation to such orders."

(11) In subsection (2)—

(a) after the first "Secretary of State" insert "or the Scottish Ministers", and

(b) after the second "Secretary of State" insert "and the Scottish Ministers".

(12) After subsection (6) insert—

"(6A) Information obtained by virtue of subsection (1A) may be disclosed by the Scottish Ministers—

(a) to the Secretary of State;

(b) to the Welsh Ministers for the purpose of enabling them to review the operation and effect in Wales of a carbon emissions reduction order or home-heating cost reduction order."

(13) In section 105 (general restrictions on disclosure of information), in subsection (3) after paragraph (a) insert—

"(aza) it is made for the purpose of facilitating the performance, by a body specified as the Administrator under an order under section 33BC or 33BD of the Gas Act 1986 or under section 41A or 41B of the Electricity Act 1989, of its functions under that section and the order;".

61 Renewable electricity incentive schemes: consultation

In the Scotland Act 1998 after section 90B (inserted by section 36) insert—

"Renewable electricity incentive schemes

90C Renewable electricity incentive schemes: consultation

(1) The Secretary of State must consult the Scottish Ministers before—

(a) establishing a renewable electricity incentive scheme that applies in Scotland, or

(b) amending such a scheme as it relates to Scotland.

(2) Subsection (1) does not apply to amendments that appear to the Secretary of State to be minor or made only for technical or administrative reasons; and the Secretary of State is not to be taken to establish or amend a scheme by exercising a power under a scheme, other than a power that is exercisable subject to any parliamentary procedure.

(3) Subsection (1) does not require the Secretary of State to consult the Scottish Ministers about any levy in connection with a renewable electricity incentive scheme.

(4) In this section a "renewable electricity incentive scheme" means any scheme, whether statutory or otherwise, that provides an incentive to generate, or facilitate the generation of, electricity from sources of energy other than fossil fuel or nuclear fuel.

This includes provision made by or under the following so far as they relate to the generation of electricity from sources of energy other than fossil fuel or nuclear fuel—

(a) sections 6 to 26 of the Energy Act 2013 (contracts for difference);

(b) sections 41 to 43 of the Energy Act 2008 (feed-in tariffs for small-scale generation of electricity);

(c) sections 32 to 32Z2 of the Electricity Act 1989 (renewables obligations or certificate purchase obligations).

(5) Where, before the commencement of this section, the Secretary of State has consulted, or is consulting, the Scottish Ministers regarding a renewable electricity incentive scheme, that consultation is to be treated as fulfilling the obligation in subsection (1)."

62 Offshore renewable energy installations

(1) The Energy Act 2004 is amended as follows.

(2) Section 95 (safety zones around renewable energy installations) is amended as follows.

(3) For subsection (1A) substitute—

"(1A) In this section and section 96 the "appropriate Minister" means the Scottish Ministers, in relation to a renewable energy installation—

(a) which is to be or is wholly in an area of Scottish waters or an area of waters in a Scottish part of a Renewable Energy Zone, and is not being or proposed to be extended outside those areas,

(b) to which paragraph (a) has ceased to apply because of an extension or proposed extension, if subsection (1B) applies, or

(c) to the extent that it is to be or is in an area of Scottish waters or an area of waters in a Scottish part of a Renewable Energy Zone, if paragraph (a) has ceased to apply because of an extension or proposed extension, and subsection (1B) does not apply,

and otherwise means the Secretary of State (subject to section 13 of the Marine and Coastal Access Act 2009, which transfers certain functions of the Secretary of State to the Marine Management Organisation).

(1B) This subsection applies if there is an agreement in force between the Secretary of State and the Scottish Ministers providing for the Scottish Ministers to be the appropriate Minister in relation to the whole of the installation.

(1C) Where subsection (1B) applies, the Scottish Ministers must consult the Secretary of State about the exercise of their functions as the appropriate Minister."

(4) In subsections (2), (3) and (7) for "Secretary of State" in each place, substitute "appropriate Minister".

(5) After subsection (4) insert—

"(4A) Before issuing a notice under this section which relates, wholly or partly, to an area outside the areas mentioned in subsection (4), the Scottish Ministers must consult the Secretary of State."

(6) Section 96 (prohibited activities in safety zones) is amended as follows.

(7) In subsection (1)(b) and (3)(b) for "Secretary of State" substitute "appropriate Minister".

(8) In subsection (8)—

(a) after "section" insert "—

(a) if made by the Secretary of State,"

(b) at the end insert ";

(b) if made by the Scottish Ministers, are subject to the negative procedure (see section 28 of the Interpretation and Legislative Reform (Scotland) Act 2010)."

(9) In section 105 (requirement to prepare decommissioning programmes) after subsection (1) insert—

"(1A) In this Chapter "appropriate Minister"—

(a) in relation to a renewable energy installation, means the Scottish Ministers—

(i) if the installation is to be or is wholly in an area of Scottish waters or an area of waters in a Scottish part of a Renewable Energy Zone, and is not being or proposed to be extended outside those areas,

(ii) if sub-paragraph (i) has ceased to apply to the installation because of an extension or proposed extension, and subsection (1B) applies, or

(iii) to the extent that the installation is to be or is in an area of Scottish waters or an area of waters in a Scottish part of a Renewable Energy Zone, if sub-paragraph (i) has ceased to apply because of an extension or proposed extension, and subsection (1B) does not apply;

and otherwise means the Secretary of State;

(b) in relation to an electric line which is or has been a related line, means—

(i) the Scottish Ministers, to the extent that the line is to be or is in an area of Scottish waters or an area of waters in a Scottish part of a Renewable Energy Zone;

(ii) otherwise, the Secretary of State.

(1B) This subsection applies to an installation if there is an agreement in force between the Secretary of State and the Scottish Ministers providing for the Scottish Ministers to be the appropriate Minister in relation to the whole of the installation.

(1C) Where subsection (1B) applies, the Scottish Ministers must consult the Secretary of State about the exercise of their functions as the appropriate Minister."

(10) In Chapter 3 (decommissioning of offshore installations), except in the provisions listed in subsection (11), for "Secretary of State" in each place substitute "appropriate Minister".

(11) The provisions not amended by subsection (10) are—

(a) sections 105(5), 106(2), 107(2), 108(7) and 111(6) (consultation of the Scottish Ministers);

(b) section 113(2) (proceedings in England and Wales or Northern Ireland).

(12) In the provisions listed in subsection (11)(a) omit "wholly or".

(13) In section 111(7) (regulations about decommissioning)—

(a) after "section" insert "—

(a) if made by the Secretary of State,"

(b) at the end insert ";

(b) if made by the Scottish Ministers, are subject to the negative procedure (see section 28 of the Interpretation and Legislative Reform (Scotland) Act 2010)."

(14) In section 112(7) (duty to inform Secretary of State: regulations)—

(a) after "section" insert "—

(a) if made by the Secretary of State,"

(b) at the end insert ";

(b) if made by the Scottish Ministers, are subject to the negative procedure (see section 28 of the Interpretation and Legislative Reform (Scotland) Act 2010)."

(15) In section 114 (interpretation of Chapter 3) in subsection (2) before the definition of "decommissioning programme" insert—

""appropriate Minister" has the meaning given by section 105(1A);".

(16) In section 192 (powers exercisable by statutory instrument) in subsection (4) after "Secretary of State" insert ", the Scottish Ministers".

(17) Schedule 16 (applications and proposals for notices under section 95) is amended as follows.

(18) For "Secretary of State" in each place, except in paragraph 7, substitute "appropriate Minister".

(19) In paragraph 9—

(a) after "Schedule" insert "—

(a) if made by the Secretary of State,"

(b) at the end insert ";

(b) if made by the Scottish Ministers, are subject to the negative procedure (see section 28 of the Interpretation and Legislative Reform (Scotland) Act 2010)."

(20) In section 13 of the Marine and Coastal Access Act 2009 (safety zones: functions under section 95 of the Energy Act 2004) omit subsection (7).

63 References to Competition and Markets Authority

In section 132(5) of the Enterprise Act 2002 (ministerial power to make references to Competition and Markets Authority: meaning of "appropriate Minister")—

(a) omit the "or" after paragraph (a), and

(b) after paragraph (b) insert—

"(c) the Scottish Ministers and the Secretary of State acting jointly; or

(d) the Scottish Ministers, the Secretary of State and one or more than one other Minister of the Crown, acting jointly."

PART 6

MISCELLANEOUS

64 Gas and Electricity Markets Authority

(1) The Utilities Act 2000 is amended as follows.

(2) In section 5 (annual and other reports of Authority)—

(a) in subsection (5) omit "and" at the end of paragraph (a) and insert—

"(aa) send a copy of the report to the Scottish Ministers, and", and

(b) after subsection (5) insert—

"(5A) The Scottish Ministers shall lay a copy of each annual report before the Scottish Parliament."

(3) After section 5 insert—

"5XA Laying of accounts before Scottish Parliament

(1) The Comptroller and Auditor General must send to the Authority, in respect of each of its accounting years, a copy of the certified accounts and report of

the Authority no later than 15th January of the financial year following that to which the accounts relate.

(2) The Authority must send to the Scottish Ministers, in respect of each of its accounting years, a copy of the certified accounts and report of the Authority no later than 31st January of the financial year following that to which the accounts relate.

(3) The Scottish Ministers must lay a copy of whatever is sent to them under subsection (2) before the Scottish Parliament.

(4) In subsections (1) and (2) "certified accounts and report" means those accounts certified under sections 5 and 7 of the Government Resources and Accounts Act 2000, and the report issued by the Comptroller and Auditor General under section 6(3)(a) of that Act."

65 Office of Communications

(1) Section 1 of the Office of Communications Act 2002 (the Office of Communications) is amended as follows.

(2) In subsection (3) after paragraph (a) insert—

"(aa) a member appointed by the Scottish Ministers;".

(3) After subsection (3) insert—

"(3A) Before appointing a member under subsection (3)(aa) the Scottish Ministers must consult the Secretary of State."

(4) In subsection (5) after "(3)(a)" insert ", (aa)".

(5) After subsection (10) insert—

"(11) Paragraphs 1 and 2 of the Schedule apply in relation to the appointment made under subsection (3)(aa) as if—

(a) any reference to the Secretary of State was to the Scottish Ministers, and

(b) after paragraph 2(6) there were inserted—

"(7) Before the Scottish Ministers remove a person from office they must consult the Secretary of State.""

(6) The Schedule to the Office of Communications Act 2002 is amended as follows.

(7) In paragraph 11(3) (accounts and audit)—

(a) omit "and" at the end of paragraph (a), and

(b) at the end of paragraph (b) insert ", and

(c) send a copy of the statement and of his report to the Scottish Ministers."

(8) After paragraph 11(3) insert—

"(4) The Scottish Ministers shall lay a copy of the statement and report sent to them under sub-paragraph (3) before the Scottish Parliament."

(9) In paragraph 12 (annual report)—

(a) in sub-paragraph (1) after "Secretary of State" insert "and the Scottish Ministers", and

(b) after sub-paragraph (3) insert—

"(4) The Scottish Ministers shall lay a copy of every report sent to them under this paragraph before the Scottish Parliament."

(10) In article 2(2) of the Public Appointments Order in Council 2014 (interpretation) in paragraph (a) of the definition of "appointing authority" after "as the case may be," insert "the Scottish Ministers,".

66 Bodies that may be required to attend before the Parliament

(1) The Scotland Act 1998 is amended as follows.

(2) After section 23 insert—

"23A Power to impose requirements on specific bodies

(1) Section 23 applies in relation to requirements imposed on a person in connection with the discharge of the functions of a body mentioned in subsection (2) in relation to Scotland with the omission of—

(a) the words after paragraph (b) in subsection (1), and

(b) subsections (2) and (6).

(2) The bodies are—

(a) the Commissioners of Northern Lighthouses,

(b) the Office of Communications, and

(c) the Gas and Electricity Markets Authority."

67 Destination of fines, forfeitures and fixed penalties

(1) The Scotland Act 1998 is amended as follows.

(2) After section 65 (payments out of the Scottish Consolidated Fund) insert—

"65A Destination of fines, forfeitures and fixed penalties

Where an Act of Parliament or subordinate legislation under an Act of Parliament requires or authorises a sum to be paid into the Consolidated Fund, and the sum appears to the Secretary of State to be a fine, forfeiture or fixed penalty, the Secretary of State may with the consent of the Treasury by regulations modify the Act or subordinate legislation so as to require or authorise the sum to be paid instead into the Scottish Consolidated Fund."

(3) In Schedule 7 (procedure for subordinate legislation), in paragraph 1(2) insert at the appropriate place—

"Section 65A	Type K"

PART 7

GENERAL

68 Subordinate legislation under functions exercisable within devolved competence

(1) Schedule 2 to the Interpretation and Legislative Reform (Scotland) Act 2010 ("the 2010 Act") (Scottish statutory instruments: transitional and consequential provision) has effect in relation to any function so far as exercisable within devolved competence by virtue of a provision of section 3, 22, 23, 24, 25, 26, 27, 31 or 50, as if references to a "pre-commencement enactment" were to—

(a) an Act passed before or in the same session as the relevant date,

(b) any other enactment passed or made before the relevant date.

(2) Schedule 3 to the 2010 Act (modification of pre-commencement enactments) has effect in relation to devolved subordinate legislation, where the function of making it is exercisable within devolved competence by virtue of a provision of section 3, 22, 23, 24, 25, 26, 27, 31 or 50, as if references to a "pre-commencement enactment" were to—

(a) an Act passed before or in the same session as the relevant date,

(b) any other enactment passed or made before the relevant date.

(3) In this section—

(a) "devolved subordinate legislation" and "enactment" have the same meaning as in Part 2 of the 2010 Act;

(b) references to the exercise of a function being within devolved competence are to be read in accordance with section 54 of the Scotland Act 1998;

(c) in relation to a provision of section 3, 22, 23, 24, 25, 26, 27, 31 or 50, the relevant date for any purpose is the date on which the provision comes into force for that purpose.

69 Transfers of property etc to the Scottish Ministers

In section 60 of the Scotland Act 1998 (transfers to the Scottish Ministers), in subsection (3), after "this Act" insert "or the Scotland Act 2016".

70 Transitional provision

(1) Nothing in a provision of this Act affects the validity of anything done by or in relation to a Minister of the Crown before the provision comes into force.

(2) Anything (including legal proceedings) which is in the process of being done by or in relation to a Minister of the Crown at the time when a provision of this Act comes into force may, so far as it relates to a function transferred to the Scottish Ministers by virtue of that provision, be continued by or in relation to the Scottish Ministers.

(3) Anything done (or which has effect as if done) by or in relation to a Minister of the Crown—

(a) which is in force when a provision of this Act comes into force, and

(b) which was done for the purposes of or in connection with a function transferred by virtue of that provision, has effect as if done by or in relation to the Scottish Ministers, so far as that is required for continuing its effect.

(4) This section applies subject to any provision made by regulations under section 71.

(5) In this section "Minister of the Crown" has the same meaning as in the Ministers of the Crown Act 1975.

71 Power to make consequential, transitional and saving provision

(1) The Secretary of State may by regulations make—

(a) such consequential provision in connection with any provision of Part 1, 3, 4, 5 or 6, or

(b) such transitional or saving provision in connection with the coming into force of any provision of Part 1, 3, 4, 5 or 6,

as the Secretary of State considers appropriate.

(2) Regulations under this section may amend, repeal, revoke or otherwise modify any of the following—

(a) an enactment or an instrument made under an enactment;

(b) a prerogative instrument;

(c) any other instrument or document.

(3) For the purposes of making provision in connection with, or with the coming into force of, a provision of Part 3, subsection (2) applies to an enactment, instrument or document whenever passed or made.

(4) Otherwise, subsection (2) applies to—

(a) an Act of Parliament passed before or in the same session as this Act;

(b) an Act of the Scottish Parliament passed, or an instrument or document made, before the end of the session in which this Act is passed.

(5) Regulations under this section may make—

(a) different provision for different purposes or cases;

(b) provision generally or for specific cases;

(c) provision subject to exceptions;

(d) provision for the delegation of functions;

(e) transitional or saving provision.

(6) Regulations under this section must be made by statutory instrument.

(7) A statutory instrument containing regulations under this section which includes provision amending or repealing any provision of primary legislation may not be made unless a draft of the instrument has been laid before and approved by a resolution of each House of Parliament.

(8) Any other statutory instrument containing regulations under this section, if made without a draft having been approved by a resolution of each House of Parliament, is subject to annulment in pursuance of a resolution of either House of Parliament.

(9) In this section—

"enactment"—

(a) includes an Act of the Scottish Parliament, and

(b) for the purposes of making provision in connection with, or with the coming into force of, a provision of Part 3, also includes a Measure or Act of the National Assembly for Wales and Northern Ireland legislation;

"prerogative instrument" means an Order in Council, warrant, charter or other instrument made under the prerogative;

"primary legislation" means—

(a) an Act of Parliament,

(b) an Act of the Scottish Parliament,

(c) a Measure or Act of the National Assembly for Wales, and

(d) Northern Ireland legislation.

(10) In Schedule 4 to the Scotland Act 1998 (enactments etc protected from modification), in paragraph 14, after "section 105" insert "or under section 71 of the Scotland Act 2016".

72 Commencement

(1) The following come into force on the day on which this Act is passed—

(a) section 1;

(b) section 36(1), (5), (6) and (9) to (12);

(c) this Part.

(2) The other provisions of section 36 come into force on the date specified under section 90B(20) of the Scotland Act 1998 (transfer date for Crown Estate scheme).

(3) Part 2 comes into force at the end of 2 months beginning with the day on which this Act is passed, subject to the provision made by that Part.

(4) The following provisions come into force on such day as the Secretary of State may appoint by regulations made by statutory instrument—

(a) sections 3 to 12;

(b) Part 3;

(c) sections 47 to 49;

(d) sections 58 to 60;

(e) section 62;

(f) section 65.

(5) Sections 20, 21 and 67 come into force on such day as the Treasury may appoint by regulations made by statutory instrument.

(6) Regulations under subsection (4) or (5) may appoint different days for different purposes.

(7) The other provisions of this Act come into force at the end of 2 months beginning with the day on which this Act is passed.

73 Short title

This Act may be cited as the Scotland Act 2016.

SCHEDULES

SCHEDULE 1

Section 18

DISAPPLICATION OF UK AGGREGATES LEVY: FURTHER AMENDMENTS

1 Part 2 of The Finance Act 2001 (aggregates levy) is amended as follows.

2 (1) Section 17 (meanings of "aggregate" and "taxable aggregate") is amended as follows.

(2) In subsection (5) (aggregate that has already been subjected to a charge) for "the United Kingdom" substitute "England, Wales or Northern Ireland".

(3) In subsection (7) (interpretation), in the definition of "highway", omit "the Roads (Scotland) Act 1984 or".

3 (1) Section 19 (commercial exploitation) is amended as follows.

(2) In subsection (5) (interpretation of references to the exploitation of aggregate in the United Kingdom) for "the United Kingdom", in both places, substitute "England, Wales or Northern Ireland".

(3) In subsection (7)(a) (mixing of aggregate in permitted circumstances) for "the United Kingdom" substitute "England, Wales or Northern Ireland".

4 In section 20(1)(a) (originating sites) for "the United Kingdom" substitute "England, Wales or Northern Ireland".

5 (1) Section 24 (levy register) is amended as follows.

(2) In subsection (3) (taxable activity for the purposes of the register) for "the United Kingdom" substitute "England, Wales or Northern Ireland".

(3) In subsection (6)(e) (registration of premises for landing of aggregate won from seabed) for "the United Kingdom", in both places, substitute "England, Wales or Northern Ireland".

6 In section 26(3) (offence of failing to provide security for levy) for "the United Kingdom" substitute "England, Wales or Northern Ireland".

7 (1) Section 30 (credit for aggregates levy) is amended as follows.

(2) In subsection (1) (cases where provision for credit may be made)—

(a) in paragraph (a) (export of aggregate) after "United Kingdom" insert ", from a place in England, Wales or Northern Ireland,", and

(b) after paragraph (a) insert—

"(aa) any of that aggregate is moved to Scotland, or to the sea adjacent to Scotland, in the form of aggregate;".

(3) After subsection (5) insert—

"(6) In subsection (1)(aa) the reference to the sea adjacent to Scotland is to so much of the territorial sea adjacent to the United Kingdom as is to be treated as adjacent to Scotland for the purposes of the Scotland Act 1998 (see section 126(2) of that Act)."

8 In section 44(a) (destination of receipts collected or received in Great Britain) for "Great Britain" substitute "England and Wales".

9 In section 48(1) (interpretation of Part 2) in the definition of "United Kingdom waters", in paragraph (a), after "Kingdom", insert ", except so much of that territorial sea as is to be treated as adjacent to Scotland for the purposes of the Scotland Act 1998 (see section 126(2) of that Act)".

10 In Schedule 4 (registration), in paragraph 8(2) (interpretation of references to taxable activity), for "the United Kingdom" substitute "England, Wales or Northern Ireland".

11 In Schedule 6 (evasion etc), in paragraph 4(1)(a) (preparations for evasion), for "the United Kingdom" substitute "England, Wales or Northern Ireland".

12 (1) Schedule 7 (information and evidence etc) is amended as follows.

(2) In paragraph 11(1) (power to take samples) for "the United Kingdom" substitute "England, Wales or Northern Ireland".

(3) In paragraph 15 (interpretation), in the definition of "connected activities" for "the United Kingdom" substitute "England, Wales or Northern Ireland".

13 In Schedule 23 to the Finance Act 2011 (data-gathering powers of HMRC), in paragraph 25(a) (relevant data-holders in relation to aggregates levy), for "the United Kingdom" substitute "England, Wales or Northern Ireland".

SCHEDULE 2

Section 44

ROADS: CONSEQUENTIAL AND RELATED PROVISION

PART 1

AMENDMENTS

Road Traffic Regulation Act 1984 (c. 52)

1 The Road Traffic Regulation Act 1984 is amended as follows.

2 (1) Section 15 (duration of orders etc under section 14) is amended as follows.

(2) In subsection (3)—

(a) for "Secretary of State", in both places, substitute "national authority", and
(b) in paragraph (b) for "that authority" substitute "the authority that made the temporary order".

(3) In subsection (4)—

(a) for "Secretary of State" substitute "national authority",
(b) omit "himself",
(c) for "he" substitute "the national authority", and
(d) for "that authority" substitute "the authority that made the temporary order".

(4) In subsections (5), (6) and (7) for "Secretary of State", in each place, substitute "national authority".

3 (1) Section 16 (supplementary provision as to orders etc under section 14) is amended as follows.

(2) In subsection (2) for "Secretary of State" substitute "national authority".

(3) In subsection (2A)—

(a) for "Secretary of State" substitute "national authority", and

(b) for "he" substitute "the national authority".

4 In section 17 (traffic regulation on special roads)—

(a) omit subsection (3ZD), and

(b) omit paragraph (b) of subsection (3A) (and the "and" before it).

5 In section 24 (Secretary of State to establish crossings on certain roads)—

(a) for "Secretary of State" substitute "national authority", and

(b) for "he", in both places, substitute "the national authority".

6 In section 25(6)(b) (meaning of "crossing" in section 25 includes a crossing established by Secretary of State under section 24)—

(a) for "Secretary of State" substitute "national authority", and

(b) for "him" substitute "the national authority".

7 In section 28 (stopping of vehicles at school crossings) for "Secretary of State", in each place, substitute "national authority".

8 (1) Section 86 (speed limits for particular classes of vehicles) is amended as follows.

(2) For "national authority" in each place substitute "relevant authority".

(3) Omit subsection (9).

9 In section 88 (temporary speed limits) for "national authority" in each place substitute "relevant authority".

10 In section 124(1) (purposes of Schedule 9 etc) in paragraphs (a) and (b) for "Secretary of State" substitute "national authority".

11 (1) Section 131 (application of road traffic enactments to Crown roads) is amended as follows.

(2) For "Secretary of State", in each place, substitute "relevant authority",

(3) In subsection (1) for "him" substitute "the relevant authority".

(4) In subsection (2)(b) for "him" substitute "the relevant authority".

(5) In subsection (2)(c) for "the authority", in both places, substitute "the appropriate Crown authority".

(6) After subsection (7) insert—

"(8) In this section "relevant authority"—

(a) in relation to functions under this section so far as exercisable within devolved competence (within the meaning of the Scotland Act 1998), means the Scottish Ministers;

(b) otherwise, means the Secretary of State."

12 (1) Section 134 (regulations) is amended as follows.

(2) In subsection (1)—

(a) for "State," substitute "State or", and

(b) omit ", or on the Ministers acting jointly,".

(3) In subsection (2)—

(a) omit "82(1)(b),",

(b) omit ", or the Ministers acting jointly as the case may be,", and

(c) for "or they think" substitute "thinks".

(4) After subsection (3) insert—

"(3A) Before making regulations under section 25, 64 or 87(1)(b) the Secretary of State must consult with the Scottish Ministers."

(5) After subsection (5) insert—

"(6) Regulations made by the Scottish Ministers under this Act (except section 86) are subject to the negative procedure.

(7) Before making regulations under section 25, 64 or 87(1)(b) the Scottish Ministers must consult with the Secretary of State.

(8) Before making regulations under this Act, except section 82(1)(b), the Scottish Ministers must consult with such representative organisations as they think fit."

13 In section 142(1) (general interpretation) omit the definition of "the Ministers".

14 (1) Part 1 of Schedule 9 (reserve powers of Secretary of State in relation to certain orders) is amended as follows.

(2) In the heading to the Part for "Secretary of State" substitute "national authority".

(3) In paragraph 1 (directions in relation to certain orders)—

(a) for "Secretary of State" substitute "national authority", and

(b) after "give to that" insert "authorised".

(4) In paragraph 2(b) (directions prohibiting certain orders)—

(a) after "prohibiting the" insert "authorised", and

(b) for "Secretary of State" substitute "national authority".

(5) In paragraph 3(1) (power of Secretary of State to make order instead of authorised authority)—

(a) for "Secretary of State" substitute "national authority", and

(b) after "as well as by the" insert "authorised".

(6) In paragraph 4 (arrangements for making order of Secretary of State effective etc)—

(a) for "Secretary of State" substitute "national authority",

(b) for "him", in each place, substitute "the national authority", and

(c) for "he", in each place, substitute "the national authority".

(7) In paragraph 6(1) (transfer of operation of parking place to local authority from Secretary of State)—

(a) for "Secretary of State", in each place, substitute "national authority", and

(b) in paragraph (b) for "he" substitute "the national authority".

(8) In paragraph 7 (variation or revocation of order by Secretary of State), in sub-paragraph (1)—

(a) for "Secretary of State" substitute "national authority", and

(b) for "he" substitute "national authority".

(9) In paragraph 8 (matters as to which Secretary of State is to be satisfied before making order)—

(a) for "Secretary of State" substitute "national authority",

(b) for "he" substitute "the national authority",

(c) for "him" substitute "the national authority", and

(d) after "discharged by the" insert "authorised".

(10) In paragraph 9 (circumstances in which paragraph 8 does not apply)—

(a) for "Secretary of State" substitute "national authority",

(b) for "he", in both places, substitute "the national authority", and

(c) for "him" substitute "the national authority".

(11) For paragraph 12A (disapplication of Article 2 of the Scotland Act 1998 (Transfer of Functions to the Scottish Ministers etc) Order 1999) substitute—

"12ZA A power conferred upon the Scottish Ministers by this Schedule, so far as it relates to the exercise of a power under this Act by virtue of section 22C, is exercisable only with the consent of the Secretary of State."

15 (1) Part 2 of Schedule 9 (consent of Secretary of State to certain orders) is amended as follows.

(2) In the heading to the Part for "Secretary of State" substitute "national authority".

(3) In paragraph 13(1) (cases where consent is required) for "Secretary of State", in each place, substitute "national authority".

(4) Paragraph 15 (Secretary of State's power to add to or remove from orders for which consent is required) is amended as follows.

(5) In sub-paragraph (1) after "authorities" insert "in England and Wales".

(6) After paragraph 15 insert—

"15A (1) The Scottish Ministers may by order add to or remove from the orders for which their consent is required by paragraph 13 such orders made by such traffic authorities in Scotland as the Scottish Ministers may specify in the order.

(2) An order under this paragraph may provide for the consent of the Scottish Ministers to be required (or not to be required) for an order for such purposes or in such circumstances as the Scottish Ministers may see fit to specify in the order under this paragraph.

(3) An order under this paragraph removing an order from the orders for which the consent of the Scottish Ministers is for the time being required is subject to the affirmative procedure.

(4) Any other order under this paragraph is subject to the negative procedure."

(7) Paragraph 16 (consent to order with modifications) is amended as follows.

(8) In sub-paragraph (1)—

(a) for "to him for his" substitute "for",

(b) after "Secretary of State" insert "or the Scottish Ministers",

(c) omit "to him", in the second place, and

(d) for "thinks" substitute "or they think".

(9) In sub-paragraph (2)—

(a) for "Where" substitute "Sub-paragraph (3) applies where",

(b) for "proposes" substitute "or the Scottish Ministers propose",

(c) after "him", in the first place, insert "or them",

(d) omit "to him", in the second place,

(e) for "he" substitute—

"(3) The Secretary of State or the Scottish Ministers", and

(f) after "him", in the third place, insert "or them".

(10) Paragraph 17 (general consent) is amended as follows.

(11) In sub-paragraph (1)—

(a) after "Secretary of State" insert "or the Scottish Ministers", and

(b) omit "his".

(12) In sub-paragraph (2) after "order" insert "of the Secretary of State".

(13) After sub-paragraph (2) insert—

"(3) Any order of the Scottish Ministers under this paragraph is subject to the negative procedure."

(14) In paragraph 18 (orders to be by statutory instrument) after "power" insert "of the Secretary of State".

16 (1) Part 3 of Schedule 9 (procedure as to certain orders) is amended as follows.

(2) In paragraph 20(1) (consultation)—

(a) for "to the Secretary of State for his" substitute "for", and

(b) omit "to the Secretary of State", in the second place.

(3) In paragraph 21 (regulations as to procedure for orders of local authorities)—

(a) for "Secretary of State", in each place, substitute "national authority",

(b) for "him", in both places, substitute "the national authority", and

(c) for "he" substitute "the national authority".

(4) In paragraph 24 (regulations as to procedure for orders of Secretary of State etc)—

(a) for "Secretary of State" substitute "national authority",

(b) in the words before paragraph (a) for "him" substitute "the national authority",

(c) in paragraph (b) for "he", in both places, substitute "the national authority", and

(d) in the words after paragraph (b) after "or" insert ", where the national authority is the Secretary of State,".

(5) Paragraph 26 (objections to exercise of reserve power under paragraph 2) is amended as follows.

(6) In sub-paragraph (1) for "Secretary of State" substitute "national authority".

(7) In sub-paragraph (2)—

(a) for "Secretary of State" substitute "national authority",

(b) for "he" substitute "the national authority", and

(c) for "him" substitute "the national authority".

17 (1) Part 4 of Schedule 9 (variation or revocation of certain orders) is amended as follows.

(2) In paragraph 28 (power to vary or revoke order not affected by related exercise of a reserve power) after "Secretary of State" insert "or the Scottish Ministers".

(3) In paragraph 29 (power to revoke an order under paragraph 7 not affected by paragraph 8)—

(a) for "Secretary of State" substitute "national authority", and

(b) omit "by him".

18 In Part 5 of Schedule 9 (consultation with traffic commissioners), in paragraph 32—

(a) for "to the Secretary of State for his", in the first place, substitute "for", and

(b) omit "to the Secretary of State for his consent", in the second place.

Road Traffic Act 1988 (c. 52)

19 In section 195 of the Road Traffic Act 1988 (regulations) after subsection (4) insert—

"(4ZA) Regulations made by the Scottish Ministers under section 20(5), 36(5) or 41(1) are subject to the negative procedure."

Road Traffic (Temporary Restrictions) Procedure Regulations 1992 (S.I. 1992/1215)

20 The Road Traffic (Temporary Restrictions) Procedure Regulations 1992 are amended as follows.

21 In regulation 9(1) (continuation of order by direction of Secretary of State) for "Secretary of State" substitute "national authority".

22 In regulation 15(5) (modification of regulation 9 in its application to Scotland) for "Secretary of State" substitute "national authority".

Zebra, Pelican and Puffin Pedestrian Crossings Regulations and General Directions 1997 (S.I. 1997/2400)

23 The Zebra, Pelican and Puffin Pedestrian Crossings Regulations and General Directions 1997 are amended as follows.

24 (1) Part 1 (the Zebra, Pelican and Puffin Pedestrian Crossings Regulations) is amended as follows.

(2) In regulation 3(1) (interpretation), in paragraph (a) of the definition of "crossing" for "Secretary of State" substitute "national authority".

(3) In paragraph 1(1)(c) of Schedule 1 (authorisation of steady light to illuminate zebra crossing globe) for "Secretary of State" substitute "national authority".

25 (1) Part 2 (the Pelican and Puffin Pedestrian Crossings General Directions 1997) is amended as follows.

(2) In direction 9 (approval of equipment relating to crossings) for "Secretary of State", in each place, substitute "national authority".

(3) In direction 10 (special directions)—

(a) in the title omit "by the Secretary of State", and

(b) in the words that follow for "Secretary of State" substitute "national authority".

National Assembly for Wales (Transfer of Functions) Order 1999 (S.I. 1999/672)

26 In Schedule 1 to the National Assembly for Wales (Transfer of Functions) Order 1999—

(a) in paragraph (e)(i) of the entry relating to the Road Traffic Regulation Act 1984 for ""the Ministers"" substitute ""the national authority"", and

(b) in paragraph (b) of the entry relating to the Road Traffic Act 1988 omit "for Wales".

Scotland Act 1998 (Transfer of Functions to the Scottish Ministers etc) Order 1999 (S.I. 1999/1750)

27 The Scotland Act 1998 (Transfer of Functions to the Scottish Ministers etc) Order 1999 is amended as follows.

28 In Schedule 1 (enactments conferring functions transferred to the Scottish Ministers) omit the entries relating to the following—

(a) the Road Traffic Regulation Act 1984;

(b) the Road Traffic (Temporary Restrictions) (Procedure) Regulations 1992;

(c) the Zebra, Pelican and Puffin Pedestrian Crossings Regulations and General Directions 1997.

29 In Schedule 3 (enactments conferring functions to be exercised subject to agreement or consultation of Scottish Ministers) omit the entries relating to the following—

(a) the Road Traffic Regulation Act 1984;

(b) the Road Traffic Act 1988, section 36(5).

Traffic Signs Regulations and General Directions 2002 (S.I. 2002/3113)

30 The Traffic Signs Regulations and General Directions 2002 are amended as follows.

31 In Part 1 (the Traffic Signs Regulations 2002), in regulation 4 (interpretation), in the definition of "primary route" for "Secretary of State" substitute "national authority".

32 (1) Part 2 (the Traffic Signs General Directions) is amended as follows.

(2) In the following directions for "Secretary of State", in each place, substitute "national authority"—

(a) direction 7(3) (signs indicating effect of statutory prohibitions);

(b) direction 28(a) (signs for migratory toad crossings);

(c) direction 38(1) (temporary signs);

(d) direction 39(6)(c) (signs for road censuses);

(e) direction 57 (approvals relating to road studs);

(f) direction 58 (supplementary provision relating to approval of road studs).

(3) In direction 56 (approval of types of sign and signals)—

(a) in paragraph (3)(a) for "Secretary of State or the Scottish Ministers" substitute "national authority", and

(b) in paragraphs (5) and (6) for "Secretary of State" substitute "national authority".

Scotland Act 1998 (Transfer of Functions to the Scottish Ministers etc) Order 2005 (S.I. 2005/849)

33 In the Schedule to the Scotland Act 1998 (Transfer of Functions to the Scottish Ministers etc) Order 2005, in the entry relating to the Road Traffic Regulation Act 1984, omit paragraph (d) (Schedule 9).

PART 2

EXERCISE OF POWERS BY AGREEMENT

Traffic Sign Powers

34 (1) Sub-paragraph (2) applies if the Secretary of State makes a statutory instrument revoking the following instruments in relation to England and Wales—

(a) the Zebra, Pelican and Puffin Pedestrian Crossing Regulations and General Directions 1997 (S.I. 1997/2400);

(b) the Traffic Signs (Temporary Obstructions) Regulations 1997 (S.I. 1997/3053);

(c) the Traffic Signs Regulations and General Directions 2002 (S.I. 2002/3113).

(2) Despite anything in section 41 or 42 or Part 1 of this Schedule, the Secretary of State may by that instrument exercise one or more of the traffic signs powers to make provision in relation to roads in Scotland (including provision revoking one or more of the instruments mentioned in sub-paragraph (1) in relation to Scotland), with the consent of the Scottish Ministers.

(3) The traffic signs powers are—

(a) the power to make regulations under section 25 of the Road Traffic Regulation Act 1984 (pedestrian crossings);

(b) the power to make regulations under section 64 of that Act (traffic signs);

(c) the power to give general directions under section 65(1) of that Act (placing of traffic signs);

(d) the power to give general directions under section 85(2) of that Act (traffic signs for indicating speed restrictions);

(e) the power to make regulations under section 36(5) of the Road Traffic Act 1988 (traffic signs: discretionary disqualification for failure to comply).

(4) The Secretary of State may exercise a power in any way by virtue of this paragraph only if the Secretary of State could have exercised it in that way but for the amendments made by sections 41 and 42 and Part 1 of this Schedule.

Powers to exempt from speed limits

35 (1) Sub-paragraph (2) applies in relation to the first statutory instrument made by the Secretary of State containing regulations under section 87(1)(b) of the Road Traffic Regulation Act 1984 as substituted by section 19 of the Road Safety Act 2006 (exemptions from speed limits: prescribed purposes and circumstances) in relation to vehicles used on roads in England.

(2) Despite anything in section 41 or 42 or Part 1 of this Schedule, the Secretary of State may by that instrument, with the consent of the Scottish Ministers—

(a) make any provision under section 87(1)(b) of the Road Traffic Regulation Act 1984 that could be made by the Scottish Ministers, and

(b) in connection with any provision made by virtue of paragraph (a), make any provision under any of the traffic signs powers mentioned in paragraph 34(3) that could be made by the Scottish Ministers.

(3) The Secretary of State may exercise a power in any way by virtue of this paragraph only if the Secretary of State could have exercised it in that way but for the amendments made by sections 41 and 42 and Part 1 of this Schedule.

Adapted and published by GRANGIS under the OGL Licence 3.0.

www.nationalarchives.gov.uk/doc/open-government-licence/version/3/

GRANGIS - UK PUBLISHING 2022.

Thank you for taking the time to leave us a review regarding this version

★★★★★

For further inquiries, contact us at:
www.grangis.com / contact@grangis.com

www.ingramcontent.com/pod-product-compliance
Lightning Source LLC
LaVergne TN
LVHW060213210926
848481LV00008B/2729